Quantum Reality, Consciousness, and Medicine Today:

THE NEW SCIENCE
OF SELF-HEALING

Yolanda Pritam Hari,
NBCTMB, CMT, QEH

BALBOA.PRESS
A DIVISION OF HAY HOUSE

Balboa Press books may be ordered through booksellers or by contacting:

Balboa Press
A Division of Hay House
1663 Liberty Drive
Bloomington, IN 47403
www.balboapress.com
1 (877) 407-4847

Because of the dynamic nature of the Internet, any web addresses or links contained in this book may have changed since publication and may no longer be valid. The views expressed in this work are solely those of the author and do not necessarily reflect the views of the publisher, and the publisher hereby disclaims any responsibility for them.

The author of this book does not dispense medical advice or prescribe the use of any technique as a form of treatment for physical, emotional, or medical problems without the advice of a physician, either directly or indirectly. The intent of the author is only to offer information of a general nature to help you in your quest for emotional and spiritual well-being. In the event you use any of the information in this book for yourself, which is your constitutional right, the author and the publisher assume no responsibility for your actions.

Scripture taken from the King James Version of the Bible.

Any people depicted in stock imagery provided by Getty Images are models, and such images are being used for illustrative purposes only. Certain stock imagery © Getty Images.

Print information available on the last page.

ISBN: 978-1-9822-3647-2 (sc)
ISBN: 978-1-9822-3646-5 (hc)
ISBN: 978-1-9822-3645-8 (e)

Library of Congress Control Number: 2019915881

Balboa Press rev. date: 10/30/2019

Welcome, Friend …

… to a personal guide for self-empowerment in what may appear to be bleak and hopeless times. The darkness around us now reflects storm clouds of our evolutionary transformation, hovering heavy with the torrents of a truth whose time has come. It's our birthright to reclaim the ability to heal ourselves. We inspire and bless others when we do.

This book is a mystery school that contains the keys.

The discoveries of quantum physics are feeding a revolution in consciousness where we use meditation to heal and transform ourselves, and then contribute peace and compassion to this world. Practical wisdom is widely available to help us "create our own reality" and "live in and as the flow." Self-regenerative, creative energy is our innate divine potential. We can realize powerful healing blessings immediately, in the bodies we have right here and now.

Exactly the knowledge we now need has been hidden for centuries, but never lost. These spiritual secrets have been preserved by mystics for thousands of years; now, modern science has revived them, giving them voice, meaning, and new life.

This book is a gift from spirit, from a long series of visions that provide us with context for the healing journey ahead. Primal intuitive knowing is foundational for life, much like a canvas contains the painting, giving it focus and space.

Herein stream pearls of wisdom for mastering positivity and accelerated transformation in our lives.

Warm Blessings,
Yolanda Pritam Hari
NBCTMB, CMT, QEH
Quiet Mind Healing ™

CONTENTS

"Those who survive the journey to the underworld earn the right to teach."

- Caroline Casey

SECTION 1

Quantum Paradigms in Health

Let's start with an overview of our newly emerging terrain.

> We are bathing in energy, we are perfused with energy,
> and it truly is a vast sea of energy that supports life within
> it, just as ocean water supports life within it.

—Dr. John Upledger, DO, OMM

****

A Call for Quantum Revolution!

*We are at a crossroads in history. Too many
people are broken or breaking.*

What if we shift our thoughts to self-transformation, and how

**our own consciousness can upgrade
our brains, hearts, and DNA?**

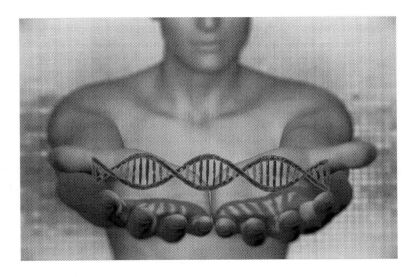

One day about a decade ago, I was reflecting on our extraordinary capacity for unimagined excellence when the phrase *quantum evolution* came to me in a sudden flash. I looked it up right away:

quantum evolution is a biology term for when species mutate within one single generation to survive. History, biologists inform us, is rich with examples of whole species' sudden mutations. DNA was rewritten instantly by environmental pressures and life's innate instinct to survive. Quantum evolution demonstrates that our DNA is miraculously hardwired for survival. Now, the new science of epigenetics adds that our thoughts have great power over our bodies, and that consciousness, not the genes themselves, directs our gene transcription (healing and evolution) throughout life.

The mind can guide us to heal and evolve beyond our conditions.

Consciousness is the key. Consciousness is life force.

Transformation begins the instant we unify our thoughts, feelings, and intentions. This is especially true in self-healing. Focus nurtures our awareness and awakens creative, regenerative energies in the body and mind. Staying present in breath and body directly activates inner power.

Life's stories are woven into our human body structure on all levels. Our cells and body tissues absorb and remember everything. It can be an arduous task to peel away the painful layers of the past. Childhood traumas and abuses, accidents and injuries that never fully healed, postural weakness and collapse from sedentary lifestyles and emotional despair, the ongoing stressors we each personally face, and then, to witness living communities lose it all to fires, earthquakes, volcanoes, and wars—***these traumatic newsreels play out in our organs, muscles, and cells, dumping stress hormones into our blood that break us down and cause pain.*** I believe we are honestly done being sick and tired all the time, poisoned by pharmaceuticals, and denied lifesaving care due to insurance limitations, misinformation, and convoluted laws. By this point, allopathy (western medicine) has done its best and is out of cards. *To survive and thrive today, we will have to take our power back!*

Reclaiming our power to heal requires attention and engaged presence. Attention asks us to stop, breathe, and feel; presence is the heart-centered awareness of *now* that results. Through presence, we become more responsive and less reactive in our lives. We feel better, and others are soothed around us. Presence helps us step forward and reach our goals. Accomplishments build our confidence, which strengthens inner knowing and trust and faith in ourselves.

Evolving consciously is a choice. Healing comes with our willingness to stop, reflect, and settle into the moment.

Through inner awareness, we get to rewrite our stories, personally and collectively. Sometimes the path unfolding looks mysteriously long. Old memories and emotions can surface. In these times, we may feel lost and really in need of compassion and support. The good news is that biology has set us up to adapt and succeed. It is a poignant window in history, and now is the time to leap. The medicine of the new paradigm is a renaissance of **consciousness.** What has emerged is the power of intention, creativity, and inner vision to take form as our lives. With conscious awareness, we assemble new outcomes from the *quantum field of possibility* instead of settling for the same old thing. Research proves conclusively that through caring for our bodies and examining our emotions and beliefs we access creativity and healing.

Evolution is our birthright, and the choice is ours to make.

The New Paradigm Unfolds

Health, peace, and compassion carry high-vibration frequencies. These energies uplift, empower, and heal.

Chaos carries lower, disorganized frequencies that cause illness by disrupting energy and form. Facing this conflict, the new paradigm teaches us to have a better relationship with ourselves. In deep and immediate ways, we are learning how to connect inwardly and hear the quiet voice of guidance in our cells. There is urgency and strong desire for these practices now. Illness is a horrifying global epidemic. The ecosystems of the human body and the earth are breaking down far faster than they can self-regulate and heal. Meanwhile, the pressures are growing ever more intense. This moment is rich with quantum evolutionary potential. The new paradigm that permeates scientific thought, consciousness research, and holistic medicine applies directly to us all.

We are the change makers of today. Our transformational tools? *Mind and heart.*

As communities and countries in a global market, we tend to be constantly busy campaigning or marketing products, so we rarely stop to process all the input we absorb. Whether or not we *realize* it, our bodies are deeply affected by pressure and stress, sudden shocks, judgments, disappointments, and noise pollution. When our nervous systems are overwhelmed, the brain short circuits and our minds and bodies default into reactivity and self-defense.

Long-term stress overpowers the voices of guidance within.

Stressful thoughts, emotions, and conditions erode life force. When chronic stresses overwhelm us, the body forgets how to heal and starts breaking down. Fears naturally arise, causing stress hormones to be dumped into the blood. Fear blocks healing. In fear, we dissociate from our bodies, hold our breaths, and deplete our adrenals. If destructive emotions are trapped inside and not felt and redirected, they continue to poison our blood.

We lose energy to subliminal messaging as well. Even when we are convinced we are not listening the media penetrates our awareness and conditions our beliefs. To recover our core sense of self, we have to center ourselves and filter out the stress. This begins with attention and breathing.

We can change any outcome with a single focused thought.

Our thoughts create energy and momentum in certain directions. This is how we attract what we imagine and think about the most. Life is a confluence of mindsets and energy patterns. As quantum physics shows, thoughts are visible as brain waves and also measurable as electromagnetic fields. Thoughts have physical reality and proven effects. The power of consciousness has enormous influence here.

Fear blocks healing, and yet our fears are culturally engrained and reinforced. Fear dominates health care and healing at the most basic level. We are essentially trained to believe we have to go to the doctor first, that the doctor is the only way, *and that to not go will bring us harm*. Through these baseline assumptions, we unconsciously surrender our intuition and freedom of choice.

Why not ask the body first?

Fear disempowers the gentle voice of Spirit alive on earth in the human heart.

Our bodies are innately programmed to self-heal. Coming into relationship with our bodies and ourselves reawakens this forgotten power.

There is great wisdom in our cells; to know that wisdom we need patience and courage to go within. Medicine in our country today is wrought with fear, panic, dread, and despair. These emotions drown our inner wisdom and degrade our health. The cost of silencing our intuition is reflected in our bodies, relationships, politics and environmental struggles now.

Relationship is all that exists. Interconnectedness is a fundamental universal law.

The sun's energy is within us; we depend on it for life. Plants provide oxygen that we give back to them as carbon dioxide so they can thrive. Mushroom spores replenish burnt forests and depleted soil. All existence is an interwoven whole. Without connection and relationship, we perish. Meditation nurtures connection, clarity, and freedom from fear. Then we are empowered with inner harmony and positive outcomes in life.

The first step of self-healing? Presence.

Presence dawns when we breathe and pay attention inside. Feelings and sensations are the body's subtle messages for us. Presence alters biochemistry so that the body can organize itself to heal.

At the atomic level, the human body is an electromagnetic conductor.

Like powerful antennas, the brain, nerves, and heart all receive input constantly from the environment, so our bodies can always sense beneath the surface of life and know intuitively what to do. In the quantum field of possibility, many options exist, which intuition will reveal. But we've been trained to disconnect from our bodies, distrust our inner knowing, and give our power away. *Medical specialists should be the last resort, not the first thought we have. Why not ask the body first?*

Let's look at the current health crisis. Prescription drug interactions and overdoses cause huge numbers of deaths every year, and there's an opioid epidemic right now because people just want to get out of pain. https://drugabuse.com/featured/overdosed/

The death statistics in this article are conservative compared to what I've heard in talks and classes over the last ten years. With big money comes the power to suppress the truth. Prescription drugs, and interactions between and among them, are serious health hazards that cause thousands of innocent deaths per year. It's common knowledge that pharmaceuticals are toxic to the liver, and most patients are on more than one drug. The liver and kidneys exhaust themselves keeping up with filtration. Then, any and all chemicals we ingest weaken cell metabolism and nerve connection between the body and the brain. Information processing slows down; fatigue sets in. Much of our country is living like this. We are conditioned that illness is normal, and we call it old age – which serves the marketing of specialists and pharmaceutical drugs. There is a safer approach. Nature is the oldest, wisest medicine there is.

The emerging paradigm for medicine is based on a more connected way of being. In the western medicine paradigm this is a foreign concept. Yet research shows that presence, self-responsibility, and body wisdom create *inner environments* conducive to healing. Acknowledging interdependence actually increases synaptic connection in the brain. Learning to trust our feelings strengthens the force field of the heart. These conscious choices restore brain coherence and harmony to the nervous and endocrine systems as a whole.

With the world speeding up, it may seem counter-intuitive to *not* just go faster ourselves. Don't most of us feel driven to keep up? But we can't balance or increase our energy if we are always pouring it out. All of nature has rhythms. Denying our bodies' rhythms and cycles is breaking us down. Holistic medicine is a lifestyle of conscious awareness and self-care based on the interconnectedness of all life. For things to change, we must reflect on what we believe and how we can live it. By taking time to breathe, pray, and inhabit our bodies, we resonate once again with the heartbeat of the earth, and our health and life naturally improve. Self-awareness and self-nurturing are important survival skills.

Neuroplasticity, Neurogenesis, and Commitment

Commitment harnesses the magnificent power of the mind.

Commitment demands our focus and attention, creating momentum in the direction of our choice. Commitment helps us learn and grow.

Commitment builds *new brain synapses*.

Learning new skills accelerates ***neurogenesis*** (the birth of new brain cells) and ***neuroplasticity*** (brain evolution based on learning).

The ***quantum sciences*** today are proving what mystics always knew: meditation and holistic lifestyle practices endow us with brain health, happiness, and a radiant electromagnetic field. Love and fear—resonance and chaos—are two very different vibrations, and the one we choose influences our health long-term. Contentment and positivity nourish us, blood and bone, while negativity dims the environment within and around us, damaging our health. Positivity allows clarity and focus, whereas with negativity, the mind doubts and wavers. Meditation allows quiet time for inner listening—and this changes the shape and function of the brain.

Countless studies have validated the power of mental focus to activate self-repair. Some will be mentioned in later sections of this book. Let's turn on these programs hidden in our DNA! It's time to claim our inborn powers to heal, evolve, and create.

****

This is an urgent moment in history. It's time to live our truth. Healing and transformation are just a mind shift away, into the heart's ways of knowing and being.

****

How Pain Roots Deep and Lasts

It starts within.

Thoughts and beliefs influence our biochemistry.

Whereas love and connection are anti-inflammatory, fear and negativity acidify the blood. Stress and anger depress our physiology and break down our immune response.

Our bodies hold the entire story of our lives.

The injuries and shocks that pile up in life get buried in the body tissue and leak out as unconscious fear and PTSD (post-traumatic stress disorder). PTSD is more common than we might think, because the pace of life often pushes us forward without ample time to process shock, loss, and pain. Even in the absence of obvious symptoms, PTSD drains our energy and weakens us because the nervous system is locked in an endless cycle of stress hormones, blood acidity, inflammation, and fatigue. Internal pressures and tensions escalate over time, while immunity and mental processes decline. Relentless stress and unaddressed trauma are the invisible root causes of pain and disease.

Emotional memories are body-based (somatic) holding patterns.

Talk therapies can't get to these places. Healing ultimately happens through the body tissue itself.

Our physical restrictions can guide us into our toxic emotions and the limiting beliefs that hold them in place. Clearing these restrictions frees the body, mind, and heart. Bodywork effectively facilitates letting go on all levels. In a short time, we can have a new lease on life.

Adapting to Change

Stage 1: Consciously Relax.

When overwhelmed by stress, the body cannot heal. To activate healing, first we must dial down the fight-or-flight response and pause the flood of stress hormones filling us.

Chronic overproduction of adrenaline and cortisol by the sympathetic nervous system burns out life force. Healing happens in parasympathetic relaxation, with slower heart, brain, and breathing rhythms; the body can rest its hypervigilance and switch its brain chemistry out of self-protection mode and into stillness and peace.

We are born knowing how to heal. Survival and adaptation are in our DNA. But the onslaught of stress and trauma in modern life triggers excess adrenal hormones that lock us in fight-or-flight mode. Chronic stress disrupts the brain and heart, causing pain, anxiety, insomnia, depression, and disease. Bodies can adapt to harsh stressors for a while, but not forever. A nervous system pedaling on high alert needs to calm down and relax in order to survive. It must be reminded how to heal.

When we spend time breathing and sitting quietly or practicing restorative yoga poses and deep relaxation, we learn to self-regulate and calm ourselves in shorter amounts of time.

There are no side effects to natural revitalizing habits, but we do need to devote regular time to practice. *Practice trains the brain and nervous system to find homeostasis and harmony.* As with any great art, attainment comes with practice.

Quieting down is an essential key to stimulate self-healing and self-repair.

If we do not establish relaxation and trust, inner conflicts persist, playing out in the body, and we find ourselves driving toward illness and chaos with both feet on the gas. The goal is to soften old fear patterns embedded in the body *and* brain. Taking time to care for ourselves is the only way through. When we let go of *doing* and learn to receive, our adrenals finally get to rest and restore.

Our primary healing task is to awaken the parasympathetic nervous system, the part that helps us rest, relax, and heal.

By focusing on this, we jump-start the natural process of self-repair. Hope returns to our hearts. We experience less pain and agitation and more contentment and inner peace.

Stage 2: Stay connected to your practice. Reset your mind *and body every day.*

To initiate connection and healing, change the channel that's running inside your head.

Choose daily practices and exercises that help you breathe, move your body, and release mental chatter and self-judgment. Brain research richly affirms what yogis have always known: mindful movement, meditation, and visualization increase neuroplasticity and reprogram our old patterns of thoughts and beliefs. I read about a study showing that two hours daily of silence increases neurogenesis by about two hundred times. Silence grows new brain circuits! When the stresses of constant stimulation are removed, the brain can rest and access growth and self-repair.

Sound also transforms the body and brain. Chanting, singing, and listening to sacred music enhances vibrational frequency and reshapes matter. We significantly alter our bodies and our brains when we sing and pray.

Sound and silence are the medicines of infinity, to which we belong.

Stage 3: Go deeper within. *The body* has a *voice!*

When pain and agitation arise, notice the distraction. Become curious. *Stop, breathe, and listen.*

What is the body saying it needs? Agree to do that.

Care for your precious body vehicle. *Now.*

Every symptom of discomfort has a source somewhere in the body that has been trying to get our attention for a long time. Once discomfort, agitation, and pain become obvious, the body is no longer whispering, but loudly calling for attention and support to balance itself out again.

We can't speed past this point with willpower. Nature takes the lead. To turn the tide of our lives, we have to reconnect. We will be stopped again and again by the body demanding that we engage in partnership with it once again.

Reconnection is a sacred act, a daily ritual that returns us to ourselves.

Harmony is the destination. Reconnection to ourselves is the path. Whatever practices bring us into sacred space are what we must do. The more familiar we grow with *not running away or checking out* when things get tough, the better we will feel.

Coherence and resilience in our bodies, brains, and hearts give us true mastery in life.

****

The evolution of consciousness requires alignment and freedom from pain.

—*Y Pritam Hari*

Quantum Reality and Self-Healing

My passions are consciousness, anatomy, and the mystery of pain.

Clearly, this work chose me.

When I was a child, people would ask me to help their pain, though I never knew why they decided to come to *me*. I noticed that most people gave up so easily and turned their lives over to doctors, resignation, and despair. This puzzled me. Aside from mandatory childhood vaccines, I never went to doctors. Knowing that our bodies can heal themselves, I have always tended to devote time and care to that instead. It just feels like the most natural thing to do. I finally understand that the shortcomings in our health and success are by-products of our conditioned beliefs.

Our culture trains us to go to the doctor first, and few people question this.

But saying we want health care to change while continuing to follow the status quo keeps us stuck right where we are.

Fear is a beast! Why not replace it with love so our cells can smile?

To me, the Western medical system seems like a hamster wheel of pain, hopelessness, prescription drugs, and disease. People are subjected to endless medical tests and procedures, and most don't find the answers they need. Then they run around, frightened and anxious, to numerous specialists, trying new drugs and getting worse. "Medical complications are expected," doctors say. "Check the fine print on the label." This trend is running rampant nationwide.

I suggest we examine our actual beliefs about healing, challenge our unconscious impulse to call the doctor first every time, and learn to rely on inner awareness and body wisdom instead.

Humans have the inborn genetic capacity for higher brain development and self-repair.

Science now shows that positive thoughts, feelings, and actions activate **regenerative genes.** Meditation, gratitude, love, and compassion are healing energies in the body. This makes sense from the standpoint of physiology. Positivity enhances the biochemical environment of our cells.

The heart's electromagnetic field is hundreds of times stronger than that of the brain.

The heart is our most powerful antenna, environmental sensor, energetic signature, and self-regulating organ. The heart knows. Heart feelings don't lie.

All living systems in nature self-regulate and self-heal.

Our bodies fluctuate constantly to adapt to stress and find balance.

Yet in Western medicine, the natural fluctuations of self-regulation are not tolerated. Instead, they are considered pathological and are immediately medicated with drugs that compromise the liver, adrenals, and gut. Not given the chance to recalibrate, the body struggles even more to adjust.

Then these same doctors pronounce conditions irreversible, insist on more and stronger drugs, and widely promote that brain and nerve tissues, once damaged, can't heal themselves.

Neuroscience research draws the opposite conclusion: neuroplasticity occurs throughout life. All body tissue—even brain and nerve cells—is replenished or repaired when given the proper environmental and nutritional support. The body knows how to heal itself.

Consciousness is our future.

Research from neuroscience and quantum physics points to the vibrational nature of reality and the super-human potential we have access to in the quantum field. In quantum reality, matter is not solid or fixed in form or location. Once we know this, the things we want come into being more readily through our focus and intention. We are not victims of fate or genes. Instead, possibilities come alive from the visions we hold.

We can learn to reset our biochemistry ourselves.

We just have to be willing to try. The new paradigm of self-responsible medicine is already in motion and actively spreading. The time is ripe.

Modern explorers like Gregg Braden, Bruce Lipton, Joe Dispenza, Lynne McTaggart, and HeartMath Institute have decades of research behind them on the consciousness of healing. Now they teach people how to mentally master self-healing on the spot.

Many among us have practiced self-healing skills quietly for years, our faith confirmed by our many successes along the way. I know people who have overcome devastating traumas by directing their meditative focus to self-heal. Yogis and shamans do it all the time.

The ancients saw Yoga as an evolutionary science of consciousness.

They invested in their self-development through meditation and attained what we still call miracles today. We too can choose to upgrade our brains and nervous systems with meditation and enhance our natural electromagnetic energy to thrive and attract what we need.

By cultivating our vibrational energy frequency to break free of the status quo and heal ourselves, we inspire others to do the same.

What could give more value to our lives today?

Consciousness is our future right now, and it's the most reliable fuel for personal transformation and global change.

Holistic medicine is growing and evolving rapidly now. Surely, sooner or later, people will tire of the hopeless, fearful runaround they've been on and will turn toward the voice within their hearts.

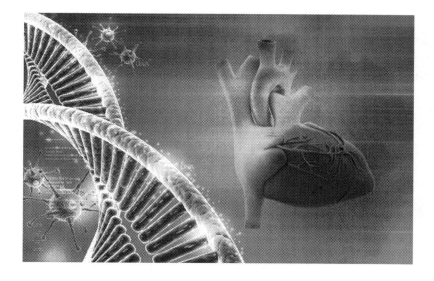

*****

I know that we are capable of beautiful dreams, great possibilities, and unspoken depths of love … that a possibility already exists in which we have ended the suffering of all creatures buy honoring the sacredness of all life.

—Gregg Braden

Neuroplasticity and Awareness

Our mindset is being stretched, more every moment now, to forge our transition into the new age.

We need new brain connections now just to conceive of how quickly science and medicine are evolving, so let's get on board!

Science is exploring what mystics have always known—how we can actively develop our awareness and our ability to influence the world with our thoughts.

The Global Consciousness Project and the Institute of Noetic Sciences have been researching the power of meditation and group consciousness on personal and political conflict since 1999. Here's what they found:

Global peace meditations have the following effects:

- increase the magnetic energy in politically unstable countries, which harmonizes the environment
- defuse conflict
- encourage communication and compassion
- create peace

These measurable energetic shifts last the entire duration of the meditation period, which indicates that peace is a conscious state of being, not merely a passing thought. ***Health, too, is a conscious state of being.***

In our DNA, there are programs to supercharge life force and capacity for self-repair. *So how do we activate healing in our bodies and the world around us?*

Heart-brain coherence, a state of biological harmony within, is the doorway to vitality, self-healing, and world peace.

Feeling compassion, meditating regularly, and breathing through the heart all create high states of coherence. Being part of a group engaged in uplifting practices amplifies the power of the results. The most perfect biofeedback mechanisms we have are the heart and the brain, yet we give them so little attention, relative to the trivialities and chaos of our lives. The heart and brain perceive everything; they are attuned to their environment through the electromagnetic field.

The heart knows the right choices to restore balance to our bodies and souls—once we learn to listen.

We live in a fortunate time. Science is proving mystical truths. Consciousness directs energy. *Where the mind moves, the energy goes.*

Consciousness becomes a healing force when we invoke feelings of trust, compassion, safety, and love. *But healing is blocked by stress, worry, anger, and fear.*

Turning inward is the key.

Meditation, spiritual connection, and altruism awaken our natural capacities for love, healing, and self-mastery.

Establishing ***heart-brain coherence*** gives us direct access to innumerable possibilities, where intention and beliefs actualize. We've been disconnected from our inner potential and living in fear for so long that we've lost our way. But we haven't lost our potential; it's just hidden by the heaviness and blindness in our hearts, which we can change. With willingness to pause and make small shifts in our focus and daily habits, we can recover intuitive self-knowledge, self-healing, and conscious engagement with life.

Many of us have awakened to the urgency now to co-create, meditate, and pray, and it is vital that we do. Our global systems are broken beyond repair, and they clearly don't have answers to pestilence, hatred, war, and disease. In fact, the way governing systems *censor research and accept corporate backing,* they seem to thrive on mistrust and disconnection. But we don't and it's no wonder so many people today are sick and depressed!

Healing is an inside job that starts within each one of us.

When we dedicate time to a relationship with ourselves based on awareness, we free ourselves to hear inner guidance and be inspired. When we uproot fear, doubt, and anger, we alter the biochemical balance of the planet, right along with our own bodies and brains.

Consciousness is the new medicine, and it defines the course of our lives, down to the micro level of our gut bacteria and genes.

Thoughts create chemicals in the brain that are released into the body, for better or for worse. Cell biologist Dr. Bruce Lipton spent thirty years researching stem cells and discovered beyond doubt that belief and state of mind alter our biochemistry and control gene transcription, which determines the destiny of our DNA.

The best medicine is what goes on between our ears and in our hearts!

Now we know how to "create our own reality." Healthy bodies come with happy hearts, centered minds, and strong electromagnetic fields.

When the Body Hurts

> [Our bodies] are not distinct from the bodies of plants and animals, with which we are involved in the cycles of feeding and the intricate companionships of ecological systems and of the spirit. They are not distinct from the earth, the sun and moon, and other heavenly bodies. It is therefore absurd to approach the subject of health piecemeal with a departmentalized band of specialists. A medical doctor uninterested in nutrition, in agriculture, in the wholesomeness of mind and spirit is as absurd as a farmer uninterested in health. Our fragmentation of this subject cannot be our cure, because it is our disease.

—Wendell Berry, *The Unsettling of America*

Presence and attention are reflected in our physiology.

Structure matters. Our body alignment—or lack of it—reflects our physical health, beliefs, and emotional states. Conscious attention to alignment reconnects us to ourselves and relieves the strain of habitual postural collapse. We develop new ways of moving and being in the body. In fact, physical realignment transforms us on all levels by resolving symptoms at their root. Postural symmetry is revitalizing and empowering.

Realigning the body frees us of memories and traumas that were locked in our tissues, causing pressure and pain. Experiencing realignment enhances our awareness, comfort, resilience, and faith in our ability to heal.

After three decades in bodywork and holistic medicine, I've noticed a pattern with body structure and blocked emotions. Misalignments initially present as low-grade tension that later escalates to anxiety, pain, illness, and then finally disease.

Misalignments can lead to many common complaints and known stages of illness: nerve compression, poor circulation, stiffness, dizziness, pain, inflammation, atrophy, and even organ failure. It's basic physiology.

Western doctors don't acknowledge or properly diagnose pain that is caused by postural strains. Bodyworkers, massage therapists, and chiropractors do.

Physical alignment processes bring us home to our bodies. Harmonizing posture, movement and breath weaves us into a dimension where intention has power: what physics calls the *quantum field of possibility.* The human body is, after all, made of all the same stuff as the trees and the stars, and it is infinitely more complex than just muscles and bones. Alignment goes well beyond 3-D; it's multidimensional and powerfully influenced by emotions. Good alignment yields more comfort in the body, and also more chances for synchronicity, spontaneous remission, and sudden bursts of creativity, clarity, and joy in life.

It's all connected. It's all one. Deep healing, like evolution, is non-linear and connects to all that is.

****

Prana, Perception, and the Medicine of Emotion

Quantum physicists and brain researchers are on the frontline, teaching us how to harness the regenerative power of the mind. This skill is the one single superpower that *could* reverse the global sickness crisis, and it's entirely possible that as enough people learn this, we will reach critical mass.

—Y Pritam Hari

Prana is the breath of life, the morning kiss that sustains everything, and the force that awakens the human soul.

Prana is the life force of the universe, as well as the breath *we* ourselves breathe. Learning to regulate breathing directly boosts our health and emotions. The yoga of breath is powerful *yet should not be done forcefully.* It actually entails softening from within. When we are stiff, tense, and angry, breathing constricts, and life flow is greatly diminished. It's so simple: the doorway to vitality and world peace is the breath. Clearly, breath connects body to mind and mind to heart.

Breath and prana *are soul itself.*

Everything we perceive and experience correlates to which neural pathways are active and which chemicals our bodies produce that then circulate through our blood.

Beneath all this lies the mystery of *prana,* our universal life force. The complexities of the human body are astounding.

Prana is the energy that sparks life and fuels evolution. *Prana* fills our bodies with energy, inspiration, and life. Perception and consciousness are expressions of *prana* too, connected into the body through breath, emotions, and thoughts. We are fully equipped in consciousness to balance and heal ourselves.

Consciousness is an energy that can be measured.

In recent years, neuroscience and brain research have surprised the world by measuring consciousness and tracking its effects. They discovered *a vibration* that interpenetrates its environment and alters the magnetic field, shaping our bodies, relationships, and health. Consciousness not only affects the world, but also could well be the formative substance of creation.

Studies find that **heart-brain coherence** produces measurable electromagnetic frequencies of harmony in the environment, as well as in our own brains.

Health is a state of harmony, not merely the absence of disease. *Heart-brain coherence* is a sustained state of harmony and inner peace. Heart-brain coherence brings our nerves to a state of rest and repair.

Heart-brain coherence carries the vibrational potency of peace.

In heart-brain coherence, there is no anger and no conflict. This is a healing state. Coherence brings healing and regeneration to all of nature.

So, science is showing us not only how to access personal healing and happier relationships, but also how to meet the political strife of our times. We are called to cultivate this more **resonant state of being** in a world gone mad, and it is an ongoing practice with each breath. By choosing to live mindfully, **we *become harmony***—the vibrational energy of peace—and the ailing world is softened by our presence.

Therein we *become* the change we wish to see.

That was Jesus's message, Gandhi's legacy, and Buddha's dream.

****

A love note to the wise: No one *really* does it alone.

Breathing and meditation move a lot of energy and can bring up body memories and symptoms for resolution. These surges can feel overwhelming at times. Find support to surf these waves! Don't struggle alone. Coaching, bodywork, and community to meditate and pray with all smooth out the rough currents.

In the process of self-transformation, our bodies introduce us to our own depths: *sweetness, rage, fear, pain, confusion and clarity*. We've all experienced some trauma, and it's in our cellular structure.

Chronic irritations from stress or injury can be like thorns stuck somewhere deep inside. The essential task is to stay present with our emotions and breath; to return to center again and again.

Bodywork, massage and energy work excel at finding the thorns and coaxing them out. More subtle styles of bodywork for pain and trauma, like CranioSacral and Biofield Therapies, are like a gentle cocoon where fear is transformed into safety through nurturing care. *Bodywork restores our relationship with ourselves, which sparks alive our self-healing power.*

We gain energy and resilience by practicing daily self-care as well. Bodywork, yoga, and plant medicine are my self-healing tools. They reconnect me with the pulse of creation, body awareness, and the guidance from within.

It takes courage to do inner work at all, as it takes courage to be alive! Going deep means there will be times we need extra help and support to stay afloat. Cleansing the old pain is the universe re-creating itself. It's foolish not to go for counseling or acupuncture or bodywork. Isolation is a self-imposed prison that ruins our health.

Only interdependence and interconnection exist in the quantum field

Through connection, all our circuits turn on, and we experience just how powerful we really are!

****

Peace starts with a smile.

—Mother Teresa

****

The Longterm Effects of Head Injuries

Head injuries are neurological traumas that initiate neurodegenerative disease. The entire nervous system is shaken, disrupted and strained.

Our culture dismisses head traumas when the assault is deep inside the brain and spine. Many times there's not a lot of blood on the surface, or maybe none at all, but there's been an impact to the brain. The **brain and spine are the central nervous system** (CNS), which connects and organizes everything about our body function and our lives. When one part is hurt, especially the brain, the entire system is compromised; and because it's invisible, it's allowed to progress. Our sense of center slowly disintegrates, and one day someone names it *degenerative disease.*

This dilemma in modern culture now is just so obvious to me, and I'd love for others to have a glimpse of what I see. There's nothing "normal" about accumulating multiple symptoms and perpetually not feeling well.

The long-term effects of brain and spinal injuries include headaches, anxiety, depression, palpitations, dizziness, pain that comes and goes, sleep disturbances, digestive distress, poor immunity, autoimmune disorders, and cognitive decline (e.g., memory loss, confusion, psychological turmoil). *This could be any one of us, or someone we know.*

I can't tell you how many of my clients forgot about some or all of their head injuries …until the point in their treatment when their bodies felt safe and ready to let it go.

For instance, here's a question for you: how many times in your life – your entire life - have you fallen, hit your head, been in a car accident, or been hit or mugged? These are all nervous system assaults. They change the shape and function of the brain. Trauma is reversible with holistic care.

Most people I know have had multiple concussions or auto accidents that they simply forgot about or minimized and then dismissed. Over and over, I see a direct correlation to their complaints. Somehow bodywork gently unravels it. There are endless protocols in today's world to help reverse and heal damage to the brain. There are foods and supplements. We must also take environmental pollution seriously and avoid toxic chemicals and medications that cross the blood-brain barrier and further injure the brain.

The human brain is the most highly refined computer system in the known universe, and our nerves are delicately tuned antennas. We calibrate thousands of physiological functions per second without ever knowing or trying, all on account of grace.

The Dalai Lama's brain research project has demonstrated the high levels of neuroplasticity in both monks and laypeople which is conditioned through meditation alone. Research subjects consistently develop steadier focus and moods, express more compassion and creativity, and experience more health and joy. These consistent results clearly indicate how meditative practices accelerate the evolution of the human brain.

On the opposite side of the fence, **head injuries, whiplash,** and **concussions** are potentially **serious brain injuries** that create **neuroplastic** changes in the brain, but in this case for the worse. These are examples of major neurological traumas that can lead to degeneration because they directly affect the structure and function of the brain.

Concussions are not neatly isolated within the skull. **Whiplash** is not just neck pain, by any means. Hard falls on the tailbone or onto the back create whiplash reactions through the entire nervous system, and the whole body is impacted.

Neurodegeneration is a progressive process, and we are seeing its various stages in populations of all ages now.

Young athletes are especially susceptible to head injury and brain damage. Early symptoms include immune system breakdown, unexplainable pain syndromes, emotional vicissitudes bordering on mental illness, and learning disabilities. ***Head injuries damage brain structure*** because they twist and tear the nerves and membrane layers of the skull. Western medicine diagnoses and treats symptoms pharmaceutically. ***They do not recognize structural injuries to the brain.*** This is a devastating error, and we now see patients of all ages with escalating complications and gradual loss of physical, emotional, mental, and cognitive function. The standard protocol is more and stronger drugs. Meanwhile, we now find integrative medical clinics dedicated to brain rehabilitation. Bodywork has also emerged as an effective non-aggressive approach. With this knowledge, we can avoid the pitfalls of progressive neurodegeneration and brain damage and steer our families toward recovery and healing.

Earlier, we mentioned the role of unconscious conditioning on our beliefs. The medical system trains us to expect degeneration and cognitive decline. *The result of* ***expecting degeneration*** *is that we experience exactly that*. Degeneration will occur. We get what we unconsciously expect. Becoming conscious and holding a broader perspective on the possibility of healing improves recovery and boosts the brain and heart. The new brain research shows that training our awareness to correct self-defeating thoughts and beliefs can reverse this tragic trajectory of neurodegenerative demise.

Consciousness is power in the new age.

But there are obstacles here.

First, most falls, crashes, whiplash incidents, and concussions are not diagnosed and treated as structural assaults to the nervous system, so they continue to progress for years. By the time patients find their way to holistic therapies, they've usually suffered with head pain, immune breakdown, and thinking problems for a long time. It can take a series of sessions to unwind. The skull is hard, but the brain and nerves are delicate and easily damaged. Skull bones often get smashed together in accidents, and overlap, putting pressure on important parts of the brain. *Proper structural treatment is subtle, sensitive work. Some therapist referral links are given at the end of the book.*

The second obstacle is the suppression of health information through corporate censorship. It's hard for us to get the word out. The revolutionary new brain therapies being taught by the Upledger and Chikly Institutes are still relatively unknown. These new manual therapies for the brain can transform suffering and degeneration with rapid efficiency. Now in the hands of several thousand bodyworkers, massage therapists, physical therapists, chiropractors, and other holistic healers, it's my prayer and vision that brain trauma be taken seriously and treated as the structural issue that it is, and that more people suffering from medical mysteries find their way to specialized bodywork and people like us. *Resources and links are provided at the end of this book to begin your search. Brain treatment is an exploding field, and each of us will be led the right way for us.*

How Brain Therapies Help Heal Pain and Disease

Our population is suffering gravely, and until recently, nobody's noticed the most obvious causes: structural alignment and brain and nerve health. My mission is to restore hope and end pain for as many people as I can.

I've studied pain and trauma for thirty years now and been trained by countless experts in the field. *The truth is bursting out of me.* I've faced many serious injuries myself exclusively with holistic medicine, meditation and spiritual practice. As a holistic coach and pain specialist, I help clients build their body knowledge, alignment, and ability to self-heal. When I reconnect people back to themselves, it heals their bodies and their brains.

Pain, dysfunction—and everything about our lives, in fact—comes down to brain and nerve health. It's now a measurable fact that stress disables the structure and function of the brain. Though the body is a mystery, its answers are revealed on the inside, and this is where we must go to heal. The new science has clearly shown that meditation can heal our brains. Natural medicine is easy to find and to practice in our lives today. *Those who come upon this book are blessed and well served.*

Modern disease reflects accumulated stresses and traumas that have gone unprocessed in our bodies for years. By addressing these at the somatic (physical and structural) level, people heal.

Illness is stress related. Whether physical, emotional, environmental, or chemical, **stress disintegrates brain circuitry.** *Overwhelm is a physiological and biochemical event that disables cell structure,* accelerating degeneration. A brain overwhelmed by chronic stress, sudden trauma, or emotional shock *will* eventually show symptoms of anxiety or depression, immune breakdown, unexplained phobias, fear, and **PTSD**. When repressed, or medicated with pharmaceuticals, these toxic energies and emotions fester and become encapsulated in the body as disease. The reason for this is simple, yet also complex.

Stress and tension interrupt cell detoxification and metabolism, which damages the organs and feeds the process of degeneration.

The effects of stress are all too common and familiar: pain, anxiety, depression, mood swings, headaches, body pain, thinking and memory problems, sleep issues, digestive trouble, metabolic disorders, chronic pain and illness, anger, self-isolation, disease, and more.

The complex part of this is the unrecognized power of destructive emotions and negative thinking to cause physical decay.

Research clearly shows that painful emotions, behaviors, and beliefs are set in our physiology *for life* by early traumas. Our bodies have held our stories, wounds, mental reactions, and emotional patterns for our whole lives. Every time we get hurt, there are physical and emotional repercussions. Each incident piles upon the last one and leaves us more limited in some way. This causes increased physical anxiety and overwhelm - fight or flight. Overwhelm leads to illness and negative self-protective behavior and thoughts. As brain injury progresses, personality changes occur.

Trauma may go unseen, but it's still a direct assault to brain and nerve cells, the heart and the soul. Trauma causes extreme stress.

Trauma reshapes the brain and nervous system, and if not treated somatically (through the body), it can cause lasting damage to the brain and destroy our natural capacity to heal. We take symptoms of pain and degeneration for granted, and dismiss them as "old age," but this assumption is misguided.

Unaddressed trauma festers within.

At the level of the brain and spinal nerves, small imbalances are huge!

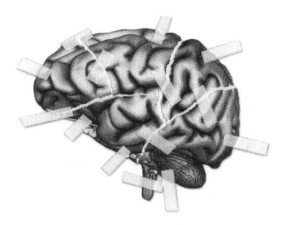

Our bodies can compensate pretty well for a long time, but at some point, cumulative stresses exceed our limits to adapt. Even our personalities and relationships degrade.

Accidents, injuries, and abuses pile up over the years, and in my clinical experience, most clients have faced numerous traumatic events alone. Many are improperly diagnosed and not treated for the traumatic injuries they sustain. Despite great efforts and expense, these patients have been unsupported by the medical system with their ongoing struggles and complaints. Their chronic conditions also cause them shame, isolation, and despair. This compounds their pain.

Enduring ceaseless pain can make us irritable, angry, ill, and even crazed as brain connections steadily break apart and recede.

Brain research now advocates holistic treatments that focus on somatic and spiritual practices. This approach is starting to trend as the most hopeful solution to our global health crisis. It's about time!

Collective cultural traumas like natural disasters, genocide, and war also remain buried in our brains and body structures as unexplained terror, phobias, and PTSD. Our own ancestral traumas also leave residues in our organs and bioenergetic fields. Heart Centered Therapy creator Alaya Chikly calls these embedded traumas "spiritual-emotional viruses," while craniosacral therapist Susan Steiner cites research showing that the epigenetic influence of emotional and generational traumas continues for at least fourteen generations. Both CranioSacral and Heart Centered Therapies reach effective resolution by treating deep emotional wounds concealed in the physical body tissue. Unwinding these threads from the physical and cellular structure helps people fully heal.

Bodywork defeats isolation and depression by increasing brain connectivity and stimulating endorphins through touch.

This is highly therapeutic.

Craniosacral and brain-lymph treatments can *reverse and heal* the effects of injury, illness, brain trauma, and emotional strain.

Bodywork therapies transform physical and emotional pain while supporting reintegration and wholeness within.

Old age and genetics are not viable excuses anymore, as Bruce Lipton's stem cell research emphatically proved. Given the right environment, our brains and bodies heal themselves every time. Focus and intention count. So let's commit to wellness instead of worry, and create our own vision of perfect health!

Rituals to Regulate Rest and Repair

An overtaxed nervous system is like a runaway train!

Physicists have discovered that the cosmos is actually spinning with ever-increasing speed, which means that time really *is* flying by incredibly fast. It's easy for our modern mantra to become "Rush, rush, rush." With so much to juggle in what feels like massively less time, our body systems are going haywire. Sleep is disturbed, our natural immunity is breaking down, our minds are full of constant worry, and the pace and pressure make it seem there's no way out.

We have to interrupt this vicious cycle in order to survive these times, let alone reestablish our quality of life.

To restore our body's natural rhythms, it is essential to allow time to rest.

No race car or airplane can stop on a dime without a crash. There's always a period of deceleration involved, and then sliding into the parking gate for service. Our living bodies need that same kind of transition. Personal rituals are a dynamic way to create an infrastructure for self-care.

Ritual doesn't have to be long and involved.

How many of us *actually have* much leisure time? Yet, without meaningful breaks in our lives, inner agitation and tension build up. Short rituals dedicated to calming and resetting your body clock can and will change how you feel. Simple healing rituals become something to look forward to outside of the stress and chaos of every day. Once our bodies learn to trust us, they remember how to heal.

My herbalism teachers insisted that busy people (like all of us!) need to block out **three hours per week as personal time off.** But *sometimes that three hours can sound like more stress than it might resolve. Then what?*

Create shorter healing rituals that make your heart scream, *"Yes!"*

Choose any simple pleasure, from a walk to an art project, taking a bubble bath, making herbal remedies for yourself, or getting a massage. First, just create the habit of stopping to attend to your health. Then, make healing dates with friends; the effects are intensified, everyone commits to showing up, and it's fun.

Start adding breaks into your calendar in order to rest and reset.

For exponential results or extreme times, create a full-day retreat. String your shorter rituals together to increase your personal retreat time when you can.

Our bodies operate on circadian rhythms, twenty-four-hour cycles of waking activity, rest, and sleep. A simple morning or evening ritual of self-care may be the best remedy for restoring your health, sleep, and peace of mind.

Here are some simple and effective time-tested ideas.

1. **Regularity: Start getting up at the same time every day, with some quiet time for yourself** before serving your family or your work. If you suffer from fatigue, it may seem contrary to force yourself out of bed even earlier than you must, but just like a good breakfast, quiet time for self-care and meditation early in the morning sets the tone for your body, health, and life.

2. **Regularity: Go to bed at the same time every night. Plan a half hour for self-care to help switch off your active mind and transition your body for sleep.** Use passive, restful yoga poses and slow breathing to this end. Or have warm, calming tea and your candlelit bubble bath at this time.

3. **Regularity: Nervine and adaptogenic herbs:** Nervines like camomile and passion flower are relaxing to the body and mind. Adaptogens like tulsi and ashwaganda balance your stress response and strengthen your nerves. Unlike drugs, herbs work synergistically inside us, directly increasing our bodies' innate ability to heal. Tinctures and teas are easy, lasting, and effective. (NB: if you have concern over alcohol-based tinctures, put your tincture drops in hot water or tea; the alcohol will evaporate and disappear.)

4. **Regularity: Go get a monthly (or weekly) massage.** Our bodies hold our life stories. Chronic stress builds up inside until it breaks us down. Stuffing down pain is a survival mechanism, but ultimately, "We can't fool Mother Nature." We all need some help and recovery time to unwind the places and ways we *hold on tight*.

5. **Regularity:** If you've been living with a nagging pain that comes and goes, and gets worse under stress, please attend to it. Constant low-level agitation indicates an overtaxed nervous system battling with fight-or-flight response ("sympathetic hyperarousal," in medical terms). Sustained physiological stress disconnects us from our bodies, which makes life feel even more unmanageable than it may already be. Bodywork and massage, structural yoga, craniosacral therapy, and chiropractic, along with breathing practices and meditation, are excellent *and highly effective approaches* to reset your body systems. Find the practitioners you resonate with; then go see them more than once! Your body and brain need time and repetition to integrate the shifts and make them last. Deep healing *can* be accomplished with regular visits over a short time. If your body likes and trusts the professional you choose, it will respond immediately without resistance and begin healing organically from within.

6. **Rituals regulate rest and repair.** *Just start somewhere.* Choose one suggestion from the above list and take charge. Dare to break the cycle of mounting stress in your life. Within a month or two, you will be surprised at how much stronger, happier, and more connected you feel!

****

Life is a long spiral, not a one-way street. Our bodies do know how to heal.

—*Yolanda Pritam Hari*

****

Yoga Therapy Tips for Stress, Panic, and Pain

In order to heal, we need to calm the fight-or-flight response long enough for our brain chemistry to change. *Healing is impossible when we are under high stress.*

1. **Stop.**
2. **Breathe.**

Chronic stress locks the nervous system on high alert, marked by high cortisol levels, anxiety, fear, shallow breathing, and even panic. It's a treadmill of pain, worry, anxiety, and adrenal fatigue. Besides, many people have respiratory issues. This is a direct cue that we need to breathe.

3. **Stop and breathe yet again.**

The **sympathetic nervous system** reacts instantaneously to threat and shock (fight, flight, or freeze). We release stress hormones like adrenaline and cortisol; overproduction of stress hormones during prolonged stress burns us out.

Breathing is the Bridge

The **parasympathetic nervous system** (where rest and healing occur) needs time to slow down and rebuild. Rhythmic breathing activates **parasympathetic relaxation** in the body and brain.

4. **Stop and breathe throughout the day. Reconnect.**

The healing process requires our presence.

There are times when pain and frustration feel relentless and disruptive physically and emotionally. The best remedy is to stop and breathe. Presence and centering are found through the breath. Presence collects our scattered energies and aligns our hearts with our intentions. Steady breathing is a self-regulating tool for the nerves.

5. **Lengthen the exhalations. This reduces stress.**

Long exhalations activate parasympathetic relaxation, conditioning the nervous system to rest, reintegrate, and self-heal. This detoxifies and strengthens the body, mind, and emotions. Exhalations also expand our breathing capacity.

Sometimes during deep breathing practices, emotions and memories can bubble up. Let them come and let them go.

For panic, blow out through your mouth. Stomp your feet. Clap your hands. Do long exhalations. Call a close friend for support. Schedule bodywork and counseling. Connection heals. Keep returning your focus to the flow of your breath.

Now meditate.

Envision love and compassion surrounding and filling you, all hearts on the planet connecting in peace. This quiets the mind and expands the sacred healing energy in our bodies.

In this way, we reinvent the whole world moment by moment. We grow deep roots and glorious blooms by overcoming adversity, illness, and pain within ourselves.

Self-healing is a profound accomplishment that empowers all of life.

photo: Yoni Mudra—gathers and carries your purpose and life force

SECTION 2

Detoxification and Life Force

Unseen Causes of Cognitive Decline and Degenerative Disease

Neurological disorders and environmental illnesses are on the increase, and people are suffering from degenerative diseases like never before. When obvious causes go unrecognized, our health complications get worse. Toxic loads are a huge threat to our health now. It's shutting down our organs. What follows is a humble introduction to the overwhelming amount of information out there now to help us reverse this epidemic.

Detoxification is a rapidly growing field of natural medicine now, one that is essential to radiant health, because we are literally bombarded by toxicants every day.

The following substances and conditions rob our brains and bodies of oxygen, energy, fluid circulation, and cell metabolism:

- **Chemicals, pesticides, and herbicides; toxic and heavy metals**
- **Harmful EMFs and atmospheric radiation**
- **Dehydration and shallow, irregular breathing**
- **Head injuries, accidents, and chronic pain**
- **Genetically modified foods**

Let's look at this in some detail.

**** ** ****

How Toxins Affect Us and What We Can Do

Chemical toxins, heavy metals, and electromagnetic smog are neurotoxic.

Neurotoxins disable the brain.

Every day, we are exposed to an infinite array of invisible neurotoxins all around us, which we inhale, ingest, or absorb through our skin. Environmental illnesses and allergies are so common now that we accept them as the norm.

Chemicals, food additives, and heavy and toxic metals are neurotoxic. *They kill brain cells.*

Environmental toxins are everywhere now. A few of the culprits are heavy metals; industrial chemicals; pesticides; herbicides; airplane fuel; car exhaust and diesel fumes; lead in car keys; lead and arsenic in cellphones; flame retardants in furniture; mercury in dental amalgams, flu shots, and other vaccines; and prescription medications with binders and additives. Even our fog and cloud cover contains highly neurotoxic combinations of heavy metals!

Neurotoxins cross the blood-brain barrier, penetrate directly into the brain, and poison the nervous system.

This causes physical and cognitive degeneration, gut microbiome disruption, anxiety, autoimmune reactions, and pain. Depending on the dose, neurotoxic substances can be absolutely deadly to the brain.

Common complaints like headaches, anxiety, brain fog, chronic fatigue, gut disturbances, pain, stiffness, and autoimmune disorders could be signs of neurotoxicity. We can reverse damage with attention to the process of self-healing.

Detoxification is essential for all of us.

Basic healthy lifestyle habits support natural detoxification and healing.

Here are some simple ideas:

Drink fresh water or warm lemon water in the morning.

In hot weather, drink cool **cucumber water** during the day. In winter, lean more on warm herbal infusions, like **nettle leaves, ginger root, and burdock root.** You'll get minerals and strengthen your immune system.

Water also helps the gut absorb water-soluble vitamins. When we're dehydrated, we become deficient in vitamins B and C. Some signs of dehydration are dry skin, headaches, constipation, and fatigue.

Eat organic. Eat lots of fresh greens.

Breathe and hydrate. *Replenish fluid levels* and oxygenate your brain with deep breathing throughout the day. *Keep life force flowing.*

If possible, avoid vaccines.

Strengthen your immune system instead.

Take time to unplug from stress and technology.

Electromagnetic smog is dangerous, especially the radiation from cell towers and the devices we wear or hold against our bodies. Like toxic and heavy metals, EMFs damage brain connections and healthy digestion, blocking metabolism and natural detoxification. EMF exposure is strongly linked to cancers and brain tumors.

Go outside into nature. Connect to the silence and the sounds.

The Earth herself emits a steady frequency of .1Hz that scientists have found synchronizes our nervous systems. This healing rhythm out in nature quickly resets our body chemistry.

Get fresh air and oxygen in your blood; sun on your back; sand and soil between your toes.

Natural places with running water like rivers, oceans, forests, and waterfalls are rich in **negative ions.** Negative ions assist detoxification, relieve inflammation, and build up our health.

Life thrives on natural fuel: sunlight, fresh air, clean water, regular exercise, and good food. But the world around us isn't supporting that right now. Our atmosphere is laden with toxic chemicals that penetrate the body and the brain.

Detoxification is essential to radiant health because we are literally bombarded every day. Chemicals, toxic and heavy metals, pollution, and noise are everywhere, and they affect us. In today's world, detoxification is not just a luxury—it's urgent.

Heavy Metals

Heavy metals damage the nervous system, the brain, and the heart.

Fluoride, chlorine, and aluminum calcify the pineal and pituitary glands, upsetting the endocrine cascades that govern life. Municipal water supplies contain these and other chemicals, which we absorb through our skin, as well as by drinking and cooking; these neuroendocrine toxins are in our toothpaste too!

Radiation and EMF's

Radiation injures our physiology. Radiation from cell phones, X-rays, cancer therapy, and microwave ovens is highly neurotoxic and immunotoxic. The scientists famed for their research on radiation and X-rays, Marie Curie and William Roentgen, both died of cancers from radiation poisoning.

EMF radiation disrupts pineal and pituitary glands, disturbing hormones, meditation, higher consciousness, and sleep cycles.

EMFs inhibit all enzymes in the body—which adversely affects metabolism and the ability to naturally detoxify.

EMFs scramble brain waves, weaken nerve signals, and disturb the gut.

Microwaves, Internet, and cell towers are the worst. Beware of 5G, which is ten thousand to one hundred thousand times the deadly radiation of the 2.5–4G we have now. There is no way to measure the cumulative assault of 5G on the body and the brain, yet corporate interests are silently and stealthily rolling it out—and we are their lab rats. No testing has been done, and none is planned.

However, growing numbers of people are developing tumors and other symptoms, such as headaches, palpitations, anxiety, and digestive distress. The effect on children and babies is exponentially greater because their brains are still developing and growing. Please don't give your children cellphones, and don't ever let your infant play with and suck on yours! It's a good dose of lead to the brain, along with the EMFs.

Smart meters are linked to brain tumors and cancers that spread fast. Smart meter radiation desynchronizes brain waves, heart rhythms, gut flora, and immunity. So does the electrical wiring in homes.

According to Dr. Ann Louse Gittleman, **"EMFs** have biological effects. Cells shut down in response, and DNA breaks … there can be blood-brain barrier leaks. EMFs also decrease melatonin production." Melatonin helps with calmness and sleep.

Toxic Chemicals

Pesticides and herbicides create many of the same symptoms of breakdown in our bodies as heavy metals and strong EMFs. Chemical toxins are not water soluble; rather, they have an affinity for fat cells. **The brain and nerves are made of cholesterol—fat.**

Herbicides and pesticides are used heavily in non-organic agriculture, and their poison shows up in high concentrations in breads, processed foods, and breast milk.

And in our brain and nerve tissue.

Testing has found that 80 percent of our food supply is laced with these poisons!

Recently, our common breakfast cereals tested high in **glyphosate,** Monsanto's extremely toxic weed killer Roundup: https://www.bbc.com/news/world-us-canada-45155788

Neurotoxins especially damage childrens' developing brains. https://www.ewg.org/release/roundup-breakfast-part-2-new-tests-weed-killer-found-all-kids-cereals-sampled

Microwave ovens emit staggeringly strong radiation, which the brain and body absorb. **Microwaves** also denature food, so the body can't digest it. This leads to gut trouble. Scientists already knew this in the 1940s, but the research was suppressed. https://www.naturalhealth365.com/microwaves-emf-pollution-2829.html

These are the things you won't hear on the evening news. Big money profits by censoring the truth.

The chemical and bioenergetic onslaught of modern life greatly stresses the human body and creates fear in the mind.

Brain toxicity makes us anxious, confused, stiff, and basically unwell.

In this **desynchronized** state, we become disempowered and succumb to fear, depression, and despair. This is why meditative awareness pays.

Body awareness alerts us to the cries for help coming from within, long before the small imbalances become disease.

Awareness also grounds us in the body, while breathing practices equalize thoughts and emotions and calm fears.

We are programmed to relinquish our true power and faith in ourselves.

We've been trained to seek experts outside ourselves and always go to the doctor *first* when we are sick.

Then doctors say there's nothing they can do, and patients instantly lose hope.

We've been **brainwashed into believing that degeneration is normal.** Meanwhile, indigenous elders and yogic masters throughout time show us this is not true. Lifelong mind training regulates emotion and brings self-renewal.

The truth can indeed set us free.

Big pharma owns the medical system, the government, and the media, and their business is driven by profit and power. Yet pharmaceuticals place such toxic loads on the body that **liver damage and kidney failure are commonly accepted side effects.**

I totally question this logic. Am I alone?

With this matrix as our foundation, it's hard to get straight answers anywhere and even harder to believe in our own ability to heal ourselves.

The new science now proves that, given the right circumstances, our bodies are genetically equipped to recalibrate, repair, and self-heal.

It may be that the toxins we absorb over time cause most of the disease on the planet today. We need to practice self-care that supports detoxification and balance day by day. With this humble and logical approach, the body and brain can relearn health and radiance again.

Detoxification is an absolute necessity, not a luxury or afterthought.

In fact, detoxification is a whole science now, readily available to us today.

With new technologies, new discoveries, and new interest in quantum medicine practices, detox methods are plentiful and close at hand.

Heavy metal toxicity causes many common symptoms, such as headaches, brain fog, and digestive disorders.

Mercury and aluminum also destroy enzymes, so our body functions are slowly disabled and eventually begin to shut down.

Heavy metals and toxic gases cross the blood-brain barrier, poison brain function, and disrupt nerve relay.

Hundreds, maybe thousands, of toxic chemicals are in the environment, and we inhale them every day.

Heavy metals include lead, mercury, aluminum, cadmium, and arsenic.

All smells go directly to the brain, which is why aromatherapy works so well.

However, since all smells go straight into the brain, time spent in toxic environments quickly damages our nerve tissue and makes us sick.

According to Dr. Dietrich Klinghardt of the Sophia Health Institute, "Mercury amalgams are the perfect antennas for cell phone and microwave radiation. There is a synergistic effect between technology and mercury residue. As [brain and body] cells degenerate, they grow … microbes, and then our immune systems break down."

He also says that viruses, including Lyme, depend on heavy metals to carry them into the brain, and that we have no choice as a species but to take detoxification seriously now.

Even fluorescent lights emit mercury gas.

We must get these poisons out of our brains and body tissue, or the suffering and fear will never end.

So what can we do?

Dr. Klinghardt says that mercury and aluminum are in our air and in vaccines, and when combined together, they can kill up to 70 percent of brain cells within a few hours. He suggests combining heavy metal detox with "agents that pull toxic metals out of the nervous system."

This heavy-metal-pulling process is called *chelation*.

Chelation therapy is a direct and effective therapeutic procedure used in functional medicine.

Chelation binds heavy metals and draws them out of the body tissue. Dr. Bruno Chikly reminds us that for effective detox, chelation alone is not enough. We must flush these poisons out through the lymph using manual therapies.

There are foods that chelate, like cilantro and medicinal mushrooms, so adding these to our diets is a good idea.

The zeolite **Clinoptilolite** is a natural filter of heavy metals – a **chelating** agent. This is a mineral we can ingest (touchstone essentials, https://thegoodinside.com/9-sneaky-ways-heavy-metals-get-into-the-body/).

Here is a link to Dr. Andrew Weil's advice on **chelation:**

https://www.drweil.com/health-wellness/balanced-living/wellness-therapies/chelation-therapy/.

Ion Cleanse Foot Bath Treatments

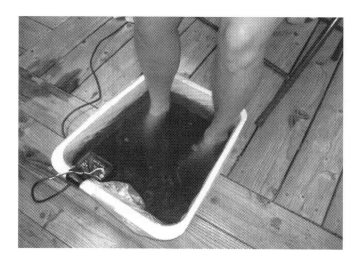

Ion cleanse detoxifying foot baths also help eliminate toxic and heavy metals and diffuse chemical loads that have accumulated in our major organs, like the liver, kidneys, brain, and nerves.

I bought my ion cleanse machine in 2008 from A Major Difference. This company, and their product, are the best: http://www.amajordifference.com?utm_source=quietmindhealing.

Having your own machine lets you detox at home on a regular basis. It helps bring down heavy metal count and defeat mold, yeast and food cravings.

We benefit from ion cleanse foot baths along with bodywork treatments. A series of ion cleanses supports heavy metal detox, and I recommend everyone consider renting or purchasing his or her own machine. Detoxification relaxes the nerves and helps the body let go.

A Major Difference invented the ion cleanse machine, and their machines exceed any other brand on the market. This company is knowledgeable, cutting edge, and thoroughly committed to customer service. *My ion cleanse machine has only needed service once in eleven years!* A Major Difference rents and sells their machines for home and professional use. This detox program is so easy to do!

Get your own ion cleanse machine to use at home. Use this link as a shortcut to research, rent, or purchase your own: http://www.amajordifference.com?utm_source=quietmindhealing.

Ion cleanses are the easiest and most effective methods of detox.

Treatment is a warm and comfortable half-hour foot bath. According to A Major Difference, independent research shows that within three consecutive treatments lasting thirty minutes each, the body's **excretion of aluminum increases 600 percent.**

By the time we become aware of pain, imbalance, or illness, chances are we've been accumulating stress and toxins for a long time. Likewise, detoxing and rebuilding our bodies may take a series of ion cleanse sessions, some dietary supplements, and some time. Having your own machine gives you freedom to care for yourself at home.

****

Sweat and Detoxification

Through sweating, the body burns toxins, which are released through the skin. We are meant to sweat regularly, but most people don't. Perhaps there's not enough time to exercise and break a sweat, or we avoid sweating because we're ashamed of messy body functions. *There are solutions even for those who don't easily sweat.*

Saunas are an excellent addition to a good workout and can also be a shortcut to a cleansing sweat. However, wood saunas mainly pull *water-soluble* toxins. Pesticides, herbicides, and heavy and toxic metals are not water soluble. They are *fat-soluble.* Chemical toxicities are serious, often fatal issues that Western medicine continues to dismiss. **Far-infrared saunas** are much more effective for detoxifying *fat-soluble* poisons.

According to Sophia Health Institute, "Japanese researchers have found that 30 percent of detoxification happens internally due the effect of the infrared rays' resonant frequencies penetrating body tissue layers. This brings about cellular detoxification, then the toxins are processed through the organs of elimination and out through the stool and urine" (https://www.sophiahi.com/effective-sauna-use-for-detoxification/).

The more we learn, the more self-empowered and self-sufficient we become. In this way, while healing ourselves, we herald the new age of self-responsible medicine and "become the change we wish to see."

****

EMFs and Detoxification

There are lots of choices on the market for neutralizing harmful EMFs. Check out the leads below, and then do some research on your own.

Invest in protection. Take breaks from your tech devices, high screen TVs, and blow dryers. Stay away from microwave ovens. Don't hold your cellphone against your head. Turn your phone to airplane mode when carrying it, and turn your wi-fi off at night.

I just purchased Gia Harmonizers from my chiropractor, plug-in EMF deflectors for each room; and last year was gifted a Q-Link pendant that I wear against my heart or wrap it around my wallet or my wrist. Both these energy medicine tools neutralize EMFs so my energy isn't always zapped. Order directly using the links below, or for personal assistance contact HYPERLINK www.tgiwellness.com;

Gia Harmonizers:

https://www.giawellness.com/85823/products/terra-gia/new-harmonizer/

Q-Links:

https://www.shopqlink.com/collections/acrylic-q-link-srt-3-pendants/products/q-link-acrylic-srt-3-pendant-black?gclid = EAIaIQobChMIqNmhnK374AIVyx-tBh2UfgpqEAQYASABEgJL4_D_BwE

Lifestyle matters.

Create a lifestyle out of all your healthy habits. Watch yourself thrive.

Energy tools offer help, support, and...energy. I've lived a holistic lifestyle and practiced yoga for nearly fifty years, so my immune system is strong. But like many people, **I am highly sensitive to chemicals and EMFs,** so I invest in energy medicine tools that are gentle enough for daily use. In addition, plant medicine is in my daily life - as foods, spices, herbal remedies and skin treatments that I make. My self-care also includes bodywork, acupuncture, and chiropractic adjustments; and I continue to study and expand my brain.

Spend time outside.

We benefit from fresh air and negative ions in nature. Breathe, walk (barefoot if possible), and look around. Feel the sun.

Condition your nervous system and build resilience.

Do yoga. Sing. Play music. Dance. Find balanced workouts. This is how we become self-empowered.

****

Magnetic and Far-Infrared Energies

The magnetic core of the earth is decreasing due to interference from man-made power sources, yet we need natural magnetic energy to survive and thrive. Without it, our health and personality disintegrate rapidly, but in highly charged magnetic fields, our health, energy and attitude skyrocket. Medical magnets are beneficial for increasing energy levels and reducing pain and fatigue. Thousands of people also report overcoming serious illnesses by using magnets and far-infrared energy healing tools. For twenty-five years, I've used magnetic and far-infrared products from Nikken. I still sleep on their sleep system to this day. The energy medicine of far-infrared and magnetic technologies supports detoxification, recovery, and energy balance.

Strong magnetic fields improve health, emotions, and energy levels.

Demagnetized environments foster aggression, depression, body pains, and extreme fatigue. In contrast, high levels of magnetic energy accelerate healing, improve sleep and metabolism, and create joy, bonding, and friendship. Far-infrared energy lessens pain and inflammation, alkalinizes the blood, and supports detoxification.

Used together, magnetic and far-infrared energies tone and balance our physiology. Special mattresses, blankets, jewelry, and clothing are available that are therapeutically infused with healing magnets and far-infrared technologies based on NASA research.

My story: "I discovered Nikken products twenty years after a serious injury, which had left me in pain and partly disabled for many years. Within six months on the sleep system, **I was able to stand and walk in the morning for the first time** since before I got hurt.

The magnetic massage roller and far-infrared joint wraps are also amazing for fast pain relief, recovery from overworking my body, and healing sprains and strains" (www.nikken.com).

Water Filters: As our municipal water supplies test higher and higher in neurotoxic chemicals, in-home filtration becomes all the more urgent. Chlorine and fluoride calcify the pineal and pituitary glands, which disrupts thinking, sleep, emotions, and hormone balance—and causes premature aging and degenerative brain shrinkage.

Our cells absorb very little hydration from city-processed, chemicalized water; however, magnetized, ionized water is fully absorbed by our cells and nourishing to the body, like a fresh running stream.

I chose Nikken countertop water filters. There are many other options in commerce now. I recently bought an easy-to-install shower filter online because my body couldn't take the chlorine any more. I was burping it!

Air filters: Airborne chemicals can be eliminated with advanced hepa-filtration systems. Many air filters sold today also generate negative ions, the "feel-good" molecules found in nature abundantly near oceans, rivers, waterfalls, forests, and trees. Negative ions boost vitality and lower inflammation.

I use Nikken air filters as well, and purchased three different models over the years. Even though they only make one model now, they still sell the filter replacements, so I have not needed to buy another air filter.

Recently Dr. Mark Hyman, who runs the Broken Brain summits, introduced the **AirDoctor** air filter and **AquaTru** water filter. He says they are the best products around. They have multiple stages of advanced filtration (https://www.aquatruwater.com https://www. airdoctorpro.com).

****

Crystals

Medicine people have used crystals for power, protection, and energization throughout history. Minerals have vitalizing effects on living systems.

Black stones like **obsidian, shungite, black kyanite, smoky quartz** (left), and **black tourmaline** (right) are best for neutralizing harmful EMFs and helping to ground the nervous system. Crystals are living minerals with their own unique electromagnetic fields. They contain and emit life force vibrations. They boost resilience and accelerate our vibratory frequency, protecting and strengthening our personal and environmental electromagnetic fields.

We will always know which ones are best for us by feel. Everything in life is about interaction and relationship.

****

Breathing and Detoxification

Clean air and fresh water are the two most vital nutrients to life.

Breathing is imperative for mind-body connection, healing, and life itself! Breath cleanses, nourishes, and energizes us. Because it sounds so simple, this simple fact is easily overlooked and ignored.

Pranayama, as the Yogic breathing practices are called, loosely translates to "the science of extending and steadying the breath." Breath reflects the health of the nervous system and the mind, and *breath regulates them both as well.* In all forms of holistic and spiritual healing, we find that the assessment and the treatment are one unified and continuous experience. Just by attending to the breath, we connect with and upgrade our physical and emotional health. This is true in bodywork too. Touch can assess conditions and treat them at the same time. Just by reading someone's craniosacral rhythm (CSR) with my hands, the person's system begins to self-regulate and heal.

Pranayama has been a very difficult path for me, and as a result, I had to go very slowly for many years. Breathwork is extremely subtle and powerful, and the human nervous system is delicate and refined.

Pranayama comes with caveats. It is unwise to jump into *pranayama* practices without calming and stabilizing the body and nervous system first. Iyengar Yoga taught me that.

I received my Iyengar Yoga teacher certification back in 1992 and taught in that system for twenty-five years. Iyengar Yoga fed my passion for anatomy, but ultimately it didn't meet my students' needs or help me heal my own disabling pain. I now teach my own system of structural yoga therapy. I still agree with the wisdom in Iyengar Yoga teachings and am very grateful. I learned a tremendous amount and got started teaching.

In Iyengar training, before **pranayama** was ever formally introduced, we prepared for several months by practicing quiet continuous breathing through the nose, restorative poses, and *shavasana* (deep relaxation).

We naturally hold our breath in times of danger, trauma, and fear.

Instinct protectively shuts us down. The process of opening again must be gentle, like a flower. If we push and pump the breath too soon, buried emotions and memories may surface all at once, overwhelming us with fear and anxiety and severely straining our nerves. This was my own challenge for years in learning *pranayama,* so I have to agree that some preparation is necessary before taking on breath retention, *kapalabati, nauli,* and other advanced techniques. The human nervous system is extremely subtle and delicate. It's too easily to get blown out.

Please, just breathe. Let go of the fancy stuff until deep breathing becomes naturally steady, relaxed, and automatic.

In the morning, sit for a while, breathing deeply in and out, and listen to the sound of the breath. Repeat this throughout the day, over and over again.

Notice when you hold your breath. Then resume breathing.

This simple practice helps shift unconscious habits of breath-holding. Breath is life, and breath moves life force. With each exhalation, we expel stress, negativity, and metabolic by-products like carbon dioxide. Long, complete exhalations instantly detoxify and calm the nerves.

Deep breathing dissolves fear.

Every form and branch of Yoga is a life science that enriches all parts of us. To breathe fully and steadily creates better health and peace of mind.

The Western mind struggles with breathing and meditation because on the surface, they are not very exciting, and our minds are very active. We tend to be impatient and start with advanced techniques right away; and we *expect* to master them right away too. This is counterproductive. To just remember to breathe, and to resume breathing when we notice we've stopped, are two small actions that will greatly transform our health and foster equanimity, friendliness, and inner peace.

****

Meditation and Chanting

Spiritual practices involving deep meditation develop the prefrontal cortex of the brain, stabilize high gamma waves, and enhance our abilities to learn, adapt, and heal.

By meditating, we cleanse, reshape, and rejuvenate the brain. Scientists find that gamma waves exponentially increase in meditators, which helps them integrate and unify diverse ideas. Gamma waves organize consciousness. This is both a physiological and electromagnetic event.

In the 1980s, the Dalai Lama initiated our current wave of brain research on meditation, and he is still involved. Tibetan monks and lamas with thousands of hours of practice demonstrate outstanding brain development, emotional stability, and immune capacity far above average. Through meditation, they've created brains that are highly evolved.

These same studies show that laypeople who meditate also make huge strides in brain development, healthy relationships, and immune capacity.

Michael Merzenich and a colleague at UCSF wrote, "We choose and sculpt how our ever-changing minds will work ... who we will be the next moment in a very real sense, and these choices are left embossed in physical form on our material selves."

Neuroplasticity occurs when we pay attention, scientists point out.

Brain science like this is poetry to my ears.

I remember reading about the monks who lived underground in Chernobyl. After the explosion, when everyone had to evacuate and many people became ill or died from the radiation, the monks were unaffected by lethal doses of radiation. *Their metabolism and immune systems were strong.* They were protected by their own powerful electromagnetic fields, cultivated through a humble lifestyle devoted to deep meditation practice.

It turns out that Indian music is also a brain science that purifies the body, emotions, and nerves, restructuring our consciousness.

There are *ragas* for every season and hour of the day and night, each divinely calculated to attune the brain and nervous system to a particular vibration and mood. Science has also found that chanting sacred mantras activates the higher brain centers by vibrating the HPA (hypothalamic-pituitary axis) every time the tongue hits the hard palate.

These are just a few highlights on how meditation aids detoxification while activating neuroplasticity and positive emotions in the brain.

****

Bodywork and Detoxification

Lack of movement creates internal stagnation. We then develop symptoms of toxicity, like **pain, inflammation, stiffness, bloating, anxiety, depression, headaches,** and much more.

Detoxification is a critical first stage to healing, radiance, and self-renewal. It lightens the chemical burden inside and opens us to receive.

Massage and bodywork actively detoxify us by moving fluids.

The body is about **75 percent water.**

Water is the medium and matrix for organs and bones. Water carries life energy into the body and toxins out.

Massage primarily flushes circulation—it moves **blood**.

Craniosacral therapy balances **cerebrospinal fluid** flow: the pure nourishing fluids within and around the brain and spinal cord.

Brain-lymph therapy addresses pain, trauma, and degeneration through the brain structure's fluid pathways, releasing cranial bone compressions and membranes' tension so the brain tissue can relax, reposition, and expand.

Manual therapy directly for the brain is a brand-new field, pioneered (to my knowledge) by Dr. Bruno Chikly, my teacher now for thirteen years.

I remember feeling a pituitary gland unwind on its stalk in my first class with Dr. Chikly and hearing his debate on which brain nuclei actually constitute the third eye. Through the years, he's introduced our minds, hearts, and hands to the vast and intimate terrain of deep brain anatomy, trauma, and pain. Before he created his **brain therapy curriculum**, his osteopathic specialty was lymph. For years, he taught his own system of **"lymphatic drainage."** Now his dedicated team of teachers covers most of those courses while he creates and teaches us this new work.

Dr. Chikly is a brilliant and fiery—yet very tender—mystic. He travels tirelessly, researching and educating on solutions for neurological disorders, degenerative brain disease, and modern struggles like autism, Lyme disease, fibromyalgia, and chronic fatigue. *Toxicity is always involved.* **Alaya Chikly,** his wife, often travels with him. Her spiritual-emotional healing system, Heart Centered Therapy, has also spread around the globe.

I've spent time studying with both of them, and it feels like *darshan* every time. *Darshan* is a Yogic term for meeting with a holy person who accelerates our transformation and growth. This couple exudes spiritual force.

Holistic healing is fundamentally a spiritual practice. Every day, we invest our presence, care, and attention in a sacred relationship with our bodies and higher selves. This yields compound interest over time. Understanding deepens. The heart expands. The body harmonizes and heals.

Our bodies always know the truth. We are sensitive cosmic antennae. The heart knows. The brain knows. The gut knows.

Turning inward, we hear that still, small voice awakening inside.

In the new **quantum reality,** infinite scenarios exist—for every situation—in any moment—once we stop, breathe, and invite guidance from within.

Meditation is the art of paying attention. It detoxifies the subconscious and purifies the heart.

Meditation makes us less reactive, which diminishes the power of fear and worry to disrupt our hearts, minds, and lives. Through meditation, we develop clarity and awareness. *This gives us choice.*

Our quantum shift in life, health, and reality could be one breath away. Presence, intention, and emotions direct the flow of our lives. We have so much more power than we ever thought.

Consciousness is the new medicine, and consciousness is alive. Consciousness can be tested and measured in labs by scientists today—and cultivated by each and every one of us willing to make a habit of meditation and self-care, and to consider the wild possibility that we *can* actually heal ourselves.

When we notice our internal cues, intuition and life force naturally increase. Detoxifying and caring for the body becomes the most natural choice, which we commit to practicing and supporting.

The innate potential to self-heal that we *each* possess is not only *natural*—it's absolutely *divine.* When we cultivate this potential through practice, we expand our awareness and access to inner power.

me with Dr. Chikly

The Four Stages of Rehabilitation

Injuries are a part of life. What follows is some sage advice to help your healing process flow toward full function again.

Until we restore symmetry and alignment to the body, we will face increased strain and limited range of motion.

Strength training alone will not accomplish this, and it may actually cause more strain.

There are many misconceptions about how best to heal from an injury and when to begin "working out" again. We tend toward impatience and expect our bodies to work way too hard, way too soon. Conscious awareness is the way into the body and all the information and gifts therein. We may not notice how we have adapted to strains, and how our injuries have distorted our posture and movement over time – yet this awareness will help us heal.

Living tissue constantly births new cells.

Bodies can be softened and molded like clay; their structure, alignment, and function can all be restored. We must be willing to consider that our living body tissue has this capacity. Then we must be willing to explore it for ourselves. All of life exists in a constant state of flux and change. Our bodies are shaped by habit and use. Scar tissue, calcium deposits, and bone fragments can all be softened and dissolved.

In successful rehabilitation, we take the body through these four stages:

    1) Release spasms
    2) Restore flexibility
    3) Restore strength
    4) Restore endurance

Most people skip to step 3 and start strength training right away. *It's too soon!*

Release spasms first. Massage, bodywork, and targeted stretching accomplish this. This step relieves pressure, restores circulation and flow (blood, lymph, cerebrospinal fluid), and stimulates stagnant nerves to fire.

Injuries and scar tissue contribute to chronic tension, pain, spasms and poor posture. Fighting spasms and forcing strained muscles to work causes further injury. The body defends by increasing tension and resisting stretch. Strained muscles have no strength until circulation returns to heal them, which doesn't happen right away. Injuries splint, which means muscles spasm and fluids collect as part of the inflammatory process. Initially, splinting protects us from further injury. For a while, there will be pain and movement limitations that allow the tissue to begin to heal. With lack of movement, blood becomes stagnant and acidic as metabolic toxins pool. At this point, it's helpful to stimulate circulation to accelerate healing. This is a sensitive process of doing the right amount; we can't force movement before the tissue knits. At first our bodies benefit from rest, massage, bodywork, gentle yoga practices, and slow, deep breathing. Then, through alignment and movement, we relieve strains and compensations from the injury before they become chronic.

Extending our exhalations activates parasympathetic nervous system relaxation, slowing down internal stress and speed so our bodies relax, unwind, and start to heal. The pressures we've accumulated are lifelong. They did not suddenly occur in a single day. Nor is the healing process generally complete in one day—although a quantum evolutionary mindset can and often does produce spontaneous healing as well. It may take us some time and practice to get to the point of spontaneous healing.

We can use our yoga practice to correct the structural problems caused by accidents and to counteract the physical demands of life and work. Alignment is a practical tool for healing and prevention, and a wonderfully productive focus for transforming mental worry into self-awareness that immediately empowers us.

Structure dictates function. Alignment counts. *We are not doomed to feel our old injuries every time it rains*. With a little more knowledge of how our bodies work, and by taking the stages of rehabilitation in order, complete and efficient rehabilitation can be right in our hands!

We are the change we wish to see.

SECTION 3

Sacred Fluids and the Physiology of Light

Water Is Life

Water is life. This is not just a slogan. It's absolute truth.

Our bodies are 75 to 80 percent water. We are fluid, not solid, by nature. Each of us is an ocean, contained within membrane sacks of fascia and skin.

Fluid movement sustains life.

Fluid movement within and across cell membranes equalizes body chemistry and initiates self-repair. Without good circulation, edema, inflammation, and atrophy result. *Fluid backup is evident—and possibly causative—in all disease.*

Life and healing happen in and through our three main body fluids: blood, lymph, and the cerebrospinal fluid (CSF).

All cells in the body breathe and filter fluids. The heart, brain, and even lymph vessels have an intrinsic pumping action. The three vital fluids—blood, lymph, and CSF—bathe and nourish the cranial membranes, the nerves, and the brain.

Blood carries oxygen and nutrients between the body and the brain. **Lymph** bathes organs, nerves, and cells and flushes metabolic waste and toxic chemicals out of the body, much like the sewer system does for our home, city, and town.

Cerebrospinal fluid cleans out and regulates the brain, spinal cord, and nervous system as a whole.

Originally, cranial osteopaths were holistic doctors who understood that the body is self-healing and that the brain "breathes" and circulates life-giving fluids. *CranioSacral Therapy evolved directly from this.*

These first osteopaths strongly sensed that cerebrospinal fluid contains and transmits physical and spiritual life force; **and that it carries this subtle essence through the human body and soul.**

> Within that cerebrospinal fluid there is an invisible element that I refer to as the "Breath of Life." … Visualize a potency, an intelligent potency, that is more intelligent than your own human mentality.
>
> —W. G. Sutherland, DO

Contemporary physician Mauro Zappaterra expounds on this with his research on the "I Am" presence in cerebrospinal fluid. Dr. Zappaterra echoes Dr. Randolph Stone's findings from half a century ago: "The soul swims in CSF." We are part and parcel of the One. The God-force flows through our bodies in the fluids that give us life, and this is science now.

Fascia and Flow: The Body's Glistening Inner Web

A tapestry of fluids resides within us. Our bodies are rivers flowing into oceans—a liquid vastness decorated with landscapes of organs and cells.

We thrive when these rivers circulate, filter, and flow.

In fact, our cells reflect and transmit light, and this light travels through our fluids. But when fluids stagnate, we lose our luminosity.

Minerals in our own bodies, and even in the bones, create the *action potential*—the electrical charge for the nerves to fire.

When nerves fire, they emit sparks of electricity.

Diffused into moving fluids, this becomes light.

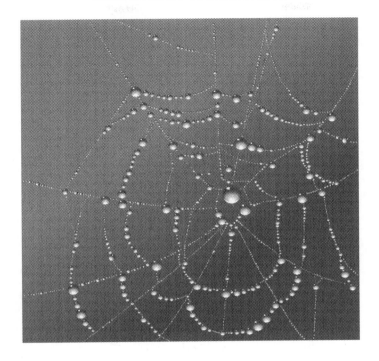

Our bodies are purified, enlivened, and illuminated by the movement of three sacred fluids: blood, lymph, and cerebrospinal fluid. Unimpeded circulation of all three fluids is essential to life. Healthy body function depends on *intercellular fluid exchange*. Fluid pathways disperse nutrients and carry away toxins and metabolic wastes.

Healthy rivers must slide around, between, and over rocks to absorb oxygen and cleanse debris. In the same way, fluids in the body filter across cell membranes and through miles of circulatory vessels and channels.

When stress, injury, illness, and inattentive habits cause strain and compression, circulation is limited. Chronic tension, postural collapse, and scar tissue all block heathy flow.

Membranes and fascia form a continuous web throughout the body, surrounding our muscles and organs and adapting to movement by bending, stretching, twisting, and folding. Fascia forms the living matrix for organs, muscles, and bones. Body structure is encased in this web of fascia, like a spider's catch is wrapped in its web. And like that spider's web, fascia threads in all directions connecting everything, and is highly responsive to movement, yet binding and strong. Fascial strains and scars lock misalignments in. When we unwind and release tension in these deeper layers of fascia, healing happens for the body, mind, and heart.

Scar Tissue

Doesn't everyone have scar tissue?

Yes.

Almost everyone.

Scar tissue is fascia that has thickened to strengthen and stabilize an injury, strain, or wound. Any physical tension or restriction we experience is held within our fascia.

Fascia is the web of connective tissue that organizes the body and suspends all of its individual parts.

Fascia is a stretchy, gooey web within us, giving our bodies shape, support, and the ability to move.

Fascia connects everywhere, weaving us into whole, integrated physical beings.

When fascia tightens, it creates pulls and tension patterns that affect all layers of the body, down into the cells.

Healthy fascia is pliable and malleable, comprising and containing our organs, muscles, and bones. However, lack of movement causes fascia to harden and knit together. We stop moving when we are injured, frightened, or working at desk jobs all day; and our fascia tightens in response, losing its structure and ability to stretch—especially at sites of injuries, surgeries, or vaccinations. Sooner or later, our joints and muscles become stiff and sore. Morning stiffness is one example of this.

But we have a choice.

Like all living body tissue, fascia can be dramatically restored.

Dr. Still, the founder of osteopathy, stated that diseases are the result of physical tension, misalignment, and restrictions that block blood, lymph, and nerve flow. Misalignments perpetuate internal strain patterns and scarring in fascia, which contributes to our ongoing stiffness and pain.

We learn organically from what we feel and experience. Bodywork is a shortcut to understanding and unwinding our anatomy. Relationship with our bodies diminishes ungrounded fears and enables inner wisdom and self-reliance to emerge.

Fascia can be reshaped by self-care, body awareness, proper hydration, good nutrition, and loving presence with oneself.

Self-repair is an inside job—of befriending and collaborating with the body, rather than pushing it around. Attention infuses our old, established habits and patterns with new energy. Change begins right away. Conscious alignment and unrestricted movement restore ease and inner peace.

Scar tissue, whether internal or visible on the skin, is the body's compassionate and valiant effort to create strength and support in broken or weakened places.

Every part of us lives inside the fascia. Like the Earth's subterranean network of mycelium, which sprouts mushrooms after heavy rains, fascia *is* the interconnected ground matrix of life.

Besides shape, support, and movement, fascia transmits nerve information and carries light.

Nerve relay is instantaneous throughout the entire body through our fascia. Because fascia is highly conductive, the body and brain receive complete downloads in a flash. The whole body instantly knows.

Luminescence: The Physiology of Light

Fascia is said to be *piezoelectric* for its magical ability to transmit information and light. We are piezoluminescent beings!

Bone is piezoelectric too. The propulsion of energy through our living tissues causes them to spark and emit a measurable electrical charge.

When our fluids are flowing, the sparks travel, and our bodies literally sparkle with light!

But when flow and life force diminish, so does that light.

A stagnant, muddy pool can't reflect light.

Health is a sacred and holy gift, to be claimed, maintained, and maximized by conscious awareness and daily self-care. Our metabolism is governed at the micro level by fluid exchange across the membranes of the cells. When our bodies have sufficient movement, hydration, and minerals, healthy fluid exchange is automatic. But when stress, lack of exercise, pharmaceuticals, environmental toxins, and processed foods strip our bodies of vitalizing minerals and precious fluids, stagnation results.

Stagnation leads to inflammation, edema, metabolic disorders, and acidosis. Disease thrives in acidic blood. We may suffer various symptoms. Yet once we recognize the actual source, we can work to reverse them with focus on lifestyle and self-care.

*Fun fact: Did you know that in a state of love and resonance, there is more space between our cells, so they can, and do, transmit more light?

Toxins and Luminescence

We underestimate how many chemicals and toxicants we are exposed to every day. They accumulate in our brains and bodies, and we gradually just adapt to living with chronic malaise.

Toxins dim our luminescence, yet pollution is everywhere. Chemicals and pesticides number in the hundreds of thousands, and every interaction between and among them creates new and worse poisons. Chemicals—which include GMO food products and pharmaceutical drugs—stress our organs, drain our energy, cause disease, and complicate its treatment. Detoxification is an important topic now.

In holistic medicine, we use detoxification to reduce inflammation and pain. It boosts our metabolism, energy levels, and brain function.

For health, joy, and inspiration to flourish, our modern lifestyle must include detoxification. Our true nature and potential are blocked by the toxic loads we accumulate inside. Clearing chemical residues from our bodies enlivens our brains, body cells, and fluid flows.

On the surface, detoxification may seem like a fad or a whole lot of work but consider the costs of being chronically ill. Sadly, we are all affected by the chemical onslaught of modern life, whether we are aware of symptoms or not. This leaves us no other real choice than to find ways to detox and rebuild our metabolism and immunity.

Neurotoxins are stored in fat cells—brain, nerve, and adipose tissue—and they accumulate over time.

Cell membranes are broken down by neurotoxins, such as environmental and atmospheric radiation, computer signals, cell towers, microwave ovens, GMO food products, glyphosate in the food chain, and chemically laden vaccines. Besides damaging brain and nerve conduction, as toxins break down cell walls, they spread through our interstitial fluids and damage internal organs. Children are especially vulnerable to all neurotoxins because their brains and immune systems are not yet fully developed. Rising rates of cancer, autism, attention deficit disorders, and neurological disorders in children have been shifting our attention to the hazards of **vaccines, environmental radiation, heavy metals, glyphosate, and genetically modified foods** as causative factors in chronic illness and disease. However, the burgeoning body of research findings has been seriously suppressed for decades by the drug and chemical companies who dominate the market and refuse to sacrifice power and profit.

Membrane damage means metabolic problems. Cells become sluggish and stop functioning.

These illnesses and their collateral damage are largely reversible through detoxification therapies, organic diet, daily hydration, yoga, mineral supplementation, and bodywork treatments. As cell metabolism is activated again, strength and life force return. It's very natural. In a clean environment, life force shines.

Here follows some fascinating science about the human body. We learned previously that **scars** are **fascia** that twists and hardens to protect the regions of our bodies that have been hurt. We tend to think of scars as the *visible* remains of cuts, wounds, and surgeries on the skin. But scars are not always visible on the surface; often they are internal, at injury and surgery sites along organs and bones.

Scars become valleys of hidden inflammation where toxins can pool. When fluid circulation is cut off, we experience unexplained stiffness and pain. In addition, our electromagnetic field—the *aura*—our personal energy signature—shrinks and becomes disorganized. Gifted healers can assess health by sensing the integrity of the electromagnetic field. In my work, once we locate scars and nerve disturbances by scanning the energy field with our hands, the pain can be diminished and dissolved.

Vaccines and injections puncture skin, causing micro-tearing of the fascia and microscopic scars. With **epidurals and spinal taps,** the scars are located within the spinal (craniosacral) membrane itself, also known as the *dura.* When the needle enters, it pierces several layers of sensitive neural tissue, which then develop inflammation, scarring, and adhesions. Scars in the dural (craniosacral) membrane compress and distort the entire nervous system. Back pain and headaches "of unknown origin" can come from this, even years after the fact. Adhesions are internal restrictions of fascial origin. Organ pain often results from fascial strains and adhesions, and also from internal ligament strains and spasms. This is all covered in Dr. Chikly's brain-lymph curriculum, which I've been studying since 2006. So many unexplainable pain problems in our population have subtle causes deep inside us. Pain begins as a quiet voice yearning to be heard, which pulsates through the oceans and rivers of life within us. To hear this voice requires a more sensitive and spiritual approach. Gentle bodywork is subtle and sensitive, affecting the formative layers of our being.

Craniosacral and lymph therapists with advanced training can feel and correct imbalances with their hands, which enables new alignment, healing, and flow.

Commitment to self-care, along with these holistic treatments, accelerates the healing process. Self-care involves how we feel about ourselves and all the ways we care for our bodies, including sufficient rest and exercise, proper diet, and time with friends. Bodywork, massage, and yoga enable deep cellular detoxification by softening physical tension and scar tissue. Craniosacral bodywork increases circulation and detoxification through the brain and spinal cord, stimulating nervous system balance. The cerebrospinal fluid filters into lymph and blood. Ionic foot baths support the efficient release of these toxins from body tissue, organs, and blood. Ion cleanse foot baths enhance detoxification by using negative ions to bind to the toxic particulates and draw them out, kind of like reverse osmosis filtration does for water.

In the healing process, detoxification is primary because we can't absorb anything until we dump out the sludge that is inside. Both children and adults can benefit greatly from a series of craniosacral sessions and ion cleanse foot baths, interspersed with massage; in fact, this may be the easiest, gentlest, and most cost-effective therapeutic approach. Whatever detox methods we choose, massage and bodywork optimize our success and help minimize any potential healing crises.

A Deeper Look at Brain Trauma, Injuries, and Scars

The body is an interconnected whole, and information travels through fascia and fluids. Tension anywhere echoes everywhere.

Fascia is the ground matrix connecting the whole body. Fascia extends from the cranial membranes out through the body, interpenetrating every vessel, organ, and cell. Injuries cause strain and pressure in the fascial network as a whole. If not released, this pressure builds, and circulation starts to shut down. Inflammation further compromises circulation and flow, and stagnation results. Overall health declines, cognitive function becomes impaired, and fatigue sets in. Slowly, the body stiffens, hardens, and develops sore and aching parts. By only looking at symptoms, doctors miss these connections completely.

Sudden trauma and chronic tension both thrust the nervous system into "sympathetic hyperarousal" (an extreme *fight-flight-freeze response),* **where stress hormones run rampant and slowly break our bodies down.**

Fascia is richly innervated, so nerve signals travel instantly through the fascial matrix. Accidents and traumas send mounting signals of alarm to the brain. *At the subconscious level, we may experience this as anxiety, panic, and PTSD.* This cycle of alarm signals and panic is perpetuated as long as the trauma remains in the body tissue irritating nerves. Chronic anxiety, physical pain, weakened immunity, and autoimmune conditions often result from the damage sustained in head injuries. Unresolved emotions like fear and rage exacerbate this reaction. By opening fluid pathways and lowering cortisol, inflammation decreases, metabolism improves, and health restores itself. The body and mind calm down.

Internal and external scars cause blood stagnation and fascial strains that distort the body and its vital fluid flows.

Healthy body tissue is resilient. When stretched, it bounces back. Injured body tissue becomes stiffly bound as a result of guarding, inflammation, lack of blood and lymph flow, and the scar tissue that then forms. This can distort posture and cause internal strain. When posture and body structure are compressed, organs become unseen sources of pain and disease. The medical term for this is "viscero-somatic referral" – pain coming from pressure in the organ. Restoring tissue resilience and addressing postural strains gives our organs the space they need to regenerate and heal. The goal is to release spasms then increase movement, elasticity and tone.

Head injuries *are brain injuries*. The subsequent inflammation and scarring limit brain circulation, regeneration, and overall health.

Brain injury goes deep. The whole nervous system suffers. **Closed-head injuries** are the least recognized and potentially the most damaging causes of pain and degeneration. These include concussions, whiplash, and falls on the tailbone—because these impacts instantly traumatize the entire spine and lodge in the body tissue somewhere. The central nervous system is violently shocked and disabled, yet this is all internal and hidden from view. Healing and regeneration are shut down by increasing brain inflammation and mounting distress in the body's fascial network.

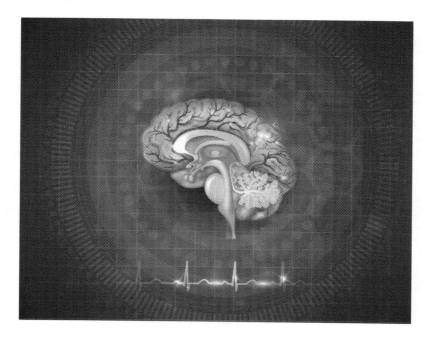

As inflammation increases, blood and lymph vessels in the brain narrow, internal pressure gradients increase, and the blood-brain barrier may rupture and leak, allowing pathogens to enter the brain and neurodegenerative processes to take hold. In the absence of healthy flow, amyloid plaques accumulate. Amyloid proteins are present in brain disorders like Alzheimer's, Parkinson's, and autism. (https://www.ncbi.nlm.nih.gov/pmc/articles/PMC3090060/)

Craniosacral and brain therapies relax the nervous system and reduce inflammation by opening cerebrospinal fluid and lymph flow around the spinal cord and brain. This puts the body directly into self-healing mode. It keeps the rivers of life circulating through us, connecting us to the flow of life itself. The nerve impulses that spark consciousness travel through our fascia and our fluids.

Touch is sacred, as is the trust that enables people to feel safe enough to unravel their bodies, emotions, and deepest concerns.

For me as a bodyworker, the craniosacral, fascial, and lymph systems are the tangible interface between matter and spirit. I understand *from personal experience* the transformative power of sensitive, subtle touch.

Touch and connection are direct solutions to the rising epidemic of isolation, depression, and pain. I believe that as our culture tires of loud advertisements, impersonal treatment, and toxic pharmaceuticals, more people will seek sensitive human touch to help them heal.

Thirty years in the field of complex pain, trauma, and rehabilitation have shown me how bodywork increases brain connections, accelerates healing, and transforms the body and the brain. But that's only the beginning.

Touch is evolutionary. It awakens the light inherent in our cells, bringing us to the point of illumination within.

The degenerative conditions we face today require subtle sensitivity to help the brain and body shift into and beyond self-repair. Sensitive hands can feel subtle structural and emotional disturbances and facilitate the freedom of release. Sensitive hands also transmit and expand light.

The primary oath in medicine is "Above all, do no harm." Manual therapies honor that oath. We create a safe and sacred container for self-healing, free of harmful pharmaceuticals and treatment complications. *Why would anyone not try skilled bodywork first?*

****

How Energy Fields Heal the Body

Cell Biology and Quantum Physics

Cell biology and quantum physics, though well founded in hard science, crossed into the realm of the mystical years ago. At the end range of all research today, the deeper findings leave us with open-ended questions on the true nature of matter and consciousness, biology and genetics, and reality itself. Newer findings abolish delineation and compartmentalization, and instead support the interconnectedness of all things. This all provides ongoing evidence for the science of how holistic medicine works.

The people silently working behind the scenes are finally being heard.

Credit and appreciation go to **Dr. Bruce Lipton** for his decades of genetic research cloning **stem cells** and his legendary discoveries of **epigenetics** and the biology of belief. Fifty years ago, Dr. Lipton left his teaching position in medical school to prove that the environment, and not our genetics, determines health and well-being. This new science, now known as epigenetics, basically explains the power we have over the expression of our genes and supports our understanding of how mind-body medicine works. Thanks to Dr. Lipton, we have fifty years of research demonstrating the power of healthy environments—which includes positive attitudes, thoughts, and expectations—over gene transcription, wellness, and the outcomes we experience in life.

Another forerunner in quantum medicine is physicist **Rupert Sheldrake,** with his pioneering research into the **morphogenetic (or morphic) field.**

Sheldrake says the morphogenetic field is like a memory in nature for how life develops and unfolds—a blueprint for each form of life.

Nerve energy is electrical, and heart energy is magnetic. Together, their resonance comprises our electromagnetic field.

Our bodies glow naturally with the biochemical energies of biological processes—life itself.

We experience this glow, this *luminescence*, as resonance in our *biofield*, The *biofield*, like the *aura*, is the electromagnetic energy signature unique to each and every living thing.

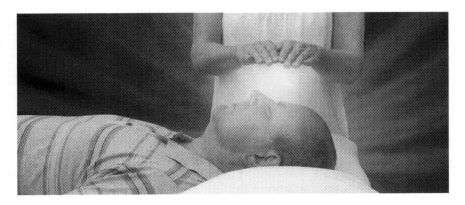

Discovered in the 1920s, the **morphogenetic field** is an organizing force in nature that carries the blueprint for how life takes form. Sheldrake teaches us that the biofield not only surrounds us, but becomes the central organizing and regenerative force for each living being.

This should be a headliner; it means we can **locate the root cause of illness by sensing it in the field** and direct and quicken healing with our hands. Subtle bodywork, such as craniosacral and lymph therapies, helps the physical body and energy field reorganize, so the client's body has a new, unbroken map to follow for self-healing.

By resolving energetic disturbances in the morphic field, the body recovers its ability to become whole.

Morphic resonance is how and why animals like lizards, salamanders, and geckoes regenerate their missing parts. When Sheldrake describes morphogenetic (or morphic) fields, he makes it all so simple to understand: https://www.youtube.com/watch?v=-3iI3JNc38Q.

****

What follows are ideas for **therapeutic self-care**. *Pick one* and stick with it for a month. See what happens. Add more as each becomes habit. *Don't stress yourself to adopt every suggestion; be realistic about your life.*

****

Simple Self-Health

It's easy to forget that simple things really work—especially in a culture addicted to noise and stimulation.

Here are a few helpful reminders.

Hydration

Drink **pure fluids** in *abundance*—the brain uses most of the water we drink. *And if we don't drink enough, the brain shorts out.*

Our blood thickens when we are dehydrated, which people may not realize. Without enough water in us, our medical tests can be full of toxic markers *precisely because* the cells can't detox. There's no fluid to move. I've known cancer patients who experienced this.

Medical doctors don't tend to mention dehydration, but if we drink enough water, the lab tests start to come out more normal. There's less use for pharmaceutical drugs.

Hydration is fundamental to every system in the body. Without it, we die.

Holistic therapies address physiology at this basic level. Water and oxygen are foundational building blocks to life. We need a steady supply of both to survive. Dehydration stresses the body and leads to inflammatory conditions. Without water, the blood thickens and acidifies. Inflammation and degenerative diseases thrive in acidic environments. Cells react to stress by releasing neurotransmitters that, in excess, cause further breakdown. Once organs and joints become painful and swollen, symptoms of degeneration can rapidly progress unless we hydrate and upgrade our self-care habits.

Sugar

Sugar and processed foods drive **degenerative** conditions.

Yet we are a sugar-driven society. Most children grow up wired. Between birthday parties, common snack foods, and monthly holidays involving chocolate, we ourselves drive the market to keep us all hooked. As a culture, we are highly dependent on stimulants. But sugar damages the pancreas, pushing the body toward metabolic disorders. Sugar also dehydrates body tissue, resulting in less circulation and more stiffness and pain. Sugar adversely affects our bones and joints. Sugar weakens the immune system as well, so we develop allergies and catch more viruses and flus.

Processed (Fake) Food

Processed food in fancy packaging is found everywhere across the globe, to our great detriment. Processing strips away the nutritional value of food, leading to chronic malnutrition and digestive disorders. Genetically modified ingredients, now present in 80 percent of the food system, further complicate the chemistry of our foodstuffs. Then we have the constant hazard in our food supply now of glyphosate, an industrial herbicide that poisons our nervous systems along with the targeted plants and weeds. Our gut microbiomes are suffering from the toxicity in our food supply. The best option for health and vitality is to choose organic whole foods and cook our own meals.

Soda and soft drinks are still a booming industry, even though research showed long ago that they can strip the paint off a car! Ingesting toxic substances makes no sense and doesn't serve our health; but it does serve corporate profits. A parade of pharmaceuticals awaits us for every complaint. Each one of us who becomes more conscious and aware helps turn our culture back toward health.

Pharmaceuticals

Pharmaceuticals may sometimes be helpful or life-saving, but most are rushed to the market without proper research and testing, and they all carry with them their own list of dangers, called side effects. Tragically, this is dismissed as the norm and amplified by the fact that most adults and many children are on multiple medications. Drug interactions can be fatal. The more chemicals that enter our bodies, the harder the liver has to work. Pharmaceutical drugs increase the liver's toxic load, leading to pain, inflammation, and disease. Once these drugs weaken the blood-brain barrier and gut lining, the brain and body become inflamed by chemicals and toxins circulating in the blood.

****

The Medicine in Water

Pure water is nature's most vital nutrient and detoxification tool.

The two most vital nutrients to life are water and oxygen—and these are the first medicines for which we need to reach. There's a classic book by Dr. Batmanghelidj, *You're Not Sick, You're Thirsty,* that promotes water as the one best single cure for all disease. Water is his medicine of choice, and his case histories will open your eyes.

To consider food and water our medicine is a life-enhancing choice.

Water is the liquid we cook with and make into medicinal soups and herbal teas. We improve our health immeasurably by adding nutritious teas, herbal infusions, and soups to our lives.

The best therapy is a preventive lifestyle approach. The following ideas integrate easily into daily life, so everyone wins. Choose *one* suggestion to try for a month. Self-care is self-repair!

Teas and Infusions

An infusion is a strong, medicinal tea made of herbs or roots. This is the most cost-effective way to nourish ourselves and help balance nutritional deficiencies.

Here's how to make an infusion: Put a handful of dried herbs in quart mason jar; fill jar with almost-boiling water, cover, and steep. For flowers, steep just a few minutes; for medicinal infusions like nettle, steep for a few hours or overnight; for roots, simmer on low flame, uncovered, for about twenty minutes or until half the liquid has evaporated. Strain and drink throughout the day.

Medicinal teas: add herbs to a pint or quart jar and cover with hot (almost boiling) water for a few minutes; then strain and drink throughout the day.

Lymph: Calendula

Nerves: Oats, oat straw, and/or milky oat top; chamomile

Sinuses and mucus membranes: Marshmallow root is a cold-steep tea, so don't use boiling water; cold will extract the slippery medicine to coat tender sinus and mucus membranes and smooth epithelial tissue. Put one handful of slivered root in a mason jar, cover with *cool* water, and steep four hours or overnight. Strain and drink throughout day; this fluid coats, soothes, and restores dry, inflamed membranes—think throat, lungs, gut, sinuses, and nasal passages.

Minerals

Minerals activate ionic exchange across cells. Without minerals, the body doesn't have enough cellular energy for muscle activity or metabolism. Minerals charge the body with (electromagnetic) life force.

Simple soup: Steam a pot of greens and save the broth; the sediment is rich in minerals from the greens. Mix broth with miso and drink, or save broth for cooking the next day.

Sea salt is one of the best sources of minerals on the planet. Sea salt contains all 98 minerals our bodies need to balance themselves. A pinch a day is all it takes. Table salt, on the other hand, is extremely damaging. It contains only two minerals, plus toxic chemicals like aluminum and plastic, which poison the brain and gut. Table salt disrupts body chemistry right away. Sea salt may cost a little more, but would we really rather sacrifice our lives for that extra $2 or $4?

Here's a link to one of my blog articles on salt: http://quietmindhealing.com/?p=1008

Lymph Activation

Lymph vessels branch out everywhere, crossing all joints. Lymph and cerebrospinal fluid are chemically similar and virtually pure. Both fluids cross paths in the brain. For good health, self-care practices include movement, exercise, massage, lymphatic and craniosacral therapies, and stretching of main lymph channels: sides of neck, collarbones, deep armpits, and groin.

Intuitive awareness is the voice of the soul.

Awareness activates self-healing. The idea is to stop and practice. Holistic treatments and self-care practices don't chase symptoms; they help balance and harmonize all body systems. By redirecting our energy inward to reconnect, *we build awareness* and experience vibrancy, regeneration, and self-healing.

Developing Subtle Awareness

* **Breathing - long exhalations** quiet mind, heart, and the parasympathetic nervous system (deep brain relaxation that leads to healing).

* **Breathing through the nose,** especially during exercise; nose breathing uses less energy and fewer muscles than mouth breathing. In cases of panic, mouth breathing—blowing the air out slowly and completely—can help neutralize the unconscious reaction to trauma.

* **Chanting:** Our bodies are *78 percent water.* Sound travels sixty times faster through water than through air. Sacred sound harmonizes matter. Singing and chanting mantras creates body, mind, and heart vibrations of healing and bliss.

* **Meditation:** First, notice your breathing rhythm; then focus on deep breathing through the nose, with long exhalations. Listen to the sound.

* **Posture:** Are you upright, comfortably seated, and present? Or tense and hyperalert? Eliminate body distractions. Find ways to be at ease.

* **Mudras:** *Hand Yoga* creates bioenergetic circuits for inner focus and whole brain integration. *(L:Pran Mudra R: Vishnu Mudra)*

* **Eye gaze *(dristi)*:** Holding eyes still helps stabilize the brain. First, relax eyes; then gently close eyes, not squeezing. Fixing the gaze between the brows or at the bottom tip of the nose influences pineal and pituitary gland balance. (NB: eye membranes connect into entire fascial system; releasing eye strain helps dissolve restrictions in the body!)

* **Blood circulation, movement, and heart rhythm:** Leg exercise, such as walking actively, pumps blood back to the heart. To passively circulate blood flow back to the heart, lying supine with legs up the wall or on a chair is basic and more restful. Our physiology is reset by inversions.

* **Yoga Asanas:** A logical sequence for an *inversions practice* would be this: shoulder opening, down dog, standing forward bends (at first, support head on block or chair), and then preparations for headstand, scorpion, handstand, and shoulder-stand. Start with the shoulder opening and forward bends first, to line up bones before asking them to bear weight. Each area of the body must be prepared for the full pose, which evolves over time. Because we lack this foundation of body awareness, yoga injuries are common. Yoga doesn't *cause* injuries. Impatience and misinformation do. It is easy now to get a teaching certificate but have little knowledge of body structure. This serves the market, but not the specific conditions and needs of newer students. People put their trust in teachers. Yoga is not simply stretching. Yoga is the science connecting consciousness in the body with the electromagnetic grid of the earth and the quantum field. The body is a vessel that carries divine Light, but asanas are not the main point. However,

patiently crafting the body-vessel allows us to carry our gifts to the end of this life's road.

If yoga is scary or painful, or if it seems too hard, ask a seasoned teacher or book a private session. Experienced professionals may cost a little more than general classes, but the cost of living with injury and fear is far higher. Structural therapists understand joint movement, rehabilitation, and pain. Our bodies don't come with manuals, but if we listen and pay attention, we will know what to do. Yoga is a practice.

In bodywork, perceptual awareness of the physical body through the biofield (aura) is what distinguishes manual therapists who "make miracles" with their touch.

We all connect first at the energetic level, which is why we are drawn immediately to some people and yet struggle with others. The relationship between our personal energy fields creates either harmony (good vibes) or disharmony (bad vibes). In disharmony we feel friction; in resonance and harmony, we experience spaciousness and love.

Manual therapies are subtle and precise. Holistic healers deeply grasp the body's innate capacity to heal itself when given the right circumstances. We nudge the natural process along. In harmonious relationship with the quantum field, healing unfolds seamlessly; the perfect blueprint for life lives there. When we organize this blueprint— which Rupert Sheldrake calls the morphogenetic field—the body's physical pathways open and flow once again, and we regain access to our infinite, inborn capacity for self-repair.

Life flows through us as itself.

Flow is life. Flow heals. Flow literally carries light. When we are flowing internally and full of light, we have the natural resilience needed to keep ourselves strong, surmount difficulties, and exude the blessings of our own radiance as light and love everywhere we go.

This is the turning point for our evolutionary leap. Through the rivers that flow within us, we become candles, then bonfires, and then North Stars twinkling, glowing, and guiding the passage across our current "dark night of the soul" back to health, wholeness, and light.

Mandate of Light   Y Pritamhari, 2016

To our angst and worry, they implored,

"Create fascial webs of consciousness
throughout the ethers,
cosmic umbrellas of light across the sky,
clear and visible galactic expanses
of brilliant stars.

"Each star, an anchor in the sparkling tapestry
of evolution,
each star, one of you."

Then they said,

"This is the non-random possibility inherent in purifying,
unwinding, and reorganizing your own body's fascial web.
You are primed for connection.
Now amplify your powers of focused intent."

Each one of us pursuing alignment within dissolves blocks and thought waves of tension, pain, and conflict from the understory of the Earth beneath our feet. This is how consciousness rebuilds heaven and Earth in every moment, through the channels of the self.

SECTION 4

Quantum Activation, Kundalini Rising, and the Physiology of Light

Quantum Medicine Is Born

The new science of self-healing is spreading rapidly now.

It has a name - *quantum medicine* - and a method - *consciousness* as the primary healing tool.

Did you ever imagine that consciousness would be recognized as real medicine by researchers and scientists today? Such is the new paradigm!

Quantum reality is best explained by the tenets of quantum physics. Anything is possible. Thoughts are real things; they vibrate at specific electromagnetic frequencies and resonate with like frequencies. All events and outcomes depend on—and mirror—our dominant thoughts and intentions. Many of us now are holding the clear intention of expressing our true gifts and destinies in life. This vision is alive in our hearts with every breath. Our commitment to the future is a palpable force.

The atmosphere feels us—and responds.

Commitment brings us to the edge of challenge, self-discovery, and self-mastery. The task is to hold focus, no matter what. The challenge is to get quiet enough to focus on and embrace that transformative potential within ourselves. We transform reality the very instant our attitude shifts toward possibilities, and we can use this energy to break free.

Since ancient times, yogis, shamans, and sages have exemplified the outer limits of consciousness evolution.

Mystics inherently understand the vibrational nature of reality, which quantum physics proved scientifically nearly a century ago. Matter is not solid. Waves and particles are always vibrating in open space and moving through black holes. In 2012, physicists located the Higgs boson particle, which they affectionately named "the God particle." Scientists allege that Higgs boson created the universe in the aftermath of the Big Bang, and physicist Stephen Hawking warned that this particle also has the power to collapse the universe without warning:

> The Higgs boson particle is so important to the Standard Model because it signals the existence of the Higgs field, an invisible energy field present throughout the universe that imbues other particles with mass. Since its discovery (in 2012), the particle has been making waves in the physics community. (https://www.livescience.com/47737-stephen-hawking-higgs-boson-universe-doomsday.html)

According to Wikipedia, "Bosons are thought to be particles which are responsible for all physical forces" and "the Higgs field is a field of energy that is thought to exist in every region of the universe" (https://simple.wikipedia.org/wiki/Higgs_field).

In my estimation, Higgs boson reflects the relationship between consciousness and the quantum field. Our thoughts, feelings, and beliefs are real energies that project out through us into the field, influencing others and shaping the world we see. By focusing consciousness and aligning our bodies, we become vortices of light—stars in the galaxy—accelerated particles of inspiration rippling out.

The energy signature each of us projects is known by these and other names: *aura, biofield, luminous body, pranic field, rainbow body.* It pulses in relationship with everything that exists.

In the last century, quantum physics has tested, measured, and validated this active vibrational frequency of light. Our brains and hearts emit strong electromagnetic signals that continually assess the environment and introduce us energetically long before we physically arrive on the scene. Our thoughts, needs, and desires extend like magnets that draw to us those very things.

We are living energy transducers.

The energy we project from the way we live our lives broadcasts our unconscious beliefs out into the world. This broadcast influences *everything* about our lives: health, illness, happiness, depression, gain, loss, connection, and disconnection.

We are tilling the soil for a grand evolutionary leap. Like great trees, the seeds of consciousness must root to thrive.

Neuroscientists and quantum physicists are hosting discussions, summits, and panels on healing through awareness. Decades ago, doctors like Deepak Chopra, Andrew Weil, Carolyn Myss, and Wayne Dyer got the engine running, and now we are seeing scientists and monks together at the helm! Meditation and awareness practices cultivate the inner terrain.

If we are paying attention, these are fascinating times.

The Chinese character for *challenge* also means *opportunity* or *choice point.* Everything here points to consciousness to decide.

Attitude and belief determine which side of the coin we see.

Stress builds resilience, just like weight training strengthens muscles and team sports develop coordination, reflexes, and mutual cooperation. We are facing a time of extreme and seemingly relentless challenge. By circumstances everywhere we look, we are being coaxed, cajoled, and compelled to meditate, to train our minds, and to build real strength and resilience within.

When we learn to breathe deeply, get quiet, and watch our thoughts, we become more and more grounded in the here and now, which is where authentic power lives.

Inner quiet brings mindful presence so that vital shifts can occur. Presence in our bodies, and in the *here and now,* is the key. When stresses are overwhelming, which they increasingly are these days, we absolutely *must* turn down the noise inside for a while.

Stopping to breathe and meditate is not a luxury. It's urgent for our survival as a species at this moment in time.

Life coach Martha Beck points out the obvious: the brain is an active supercomputer. When it shorts out, we have to **stop and reboot.**

When our computers get too hot, we power them down, rest them until they cool, and then restart them. Our brains run a lot of electricity too, and our wires can overheat, short out, break, and fray, like in any machine. Information overload quite literally overwhelms brain circuits, creating way too much heat. Brain hyperactivity burns nerve endings and damages the myelin sheath. Myelin coats nerves to speed conduction between the body and brain.

Myelin facilitates nerve transmission.

When myelin wears thin or gets damaged, as it does in MS (multiple sclerosis), Alzheimer's, and other neurodegenerative autoimmune diseases, communications between parts of the body break down. Then, degenerative brain and nerve conditions can quickly progress.

Neuroplasticity Is Natural

Neuroplasticity, the brain's ability to rewire according to need, happens throughout our lives. Whether for better or for worse, the brain can be trained to expand into possibility or contract into fear. The outcome is largely up to us.

In the modern world, trying to "keep up with everything" and "get it all done" are no longer options. It's sheer self-delusion to imagine that we can. With the frantic onslaught of demands on our attention and the brain circuitry we were given, a state of being overwhelmed is common. We have to slow the input down. Finding center is the first step in healing. We regain our ground when we stop to reboot. This is called self-regulation. *Self-regulation strengthens our adaptability.*

Adaptability and learning are *neuroplastic* responses; the brain changes shape and function. ***Learning increases neuroplasticity.*** New synaptic connections are formed, which expand communication in the brain. Better communication brings emotional integration; connectivity nourishes our life force.

In fact, science has discovered a fourth brain, the social brain, which enables cooperation, empathy, and altruism. The social brain enables direct, non-conscious connection between us by way of brain signaling, and is vital to bonding and brain development. In the absence of social support, the brain shrinks and loses connectivity. Social brain circuits connect us to the feelings of others in order to expand our positive resonance and sphere of influence. This occurs through a process physics calls *quantum entanglement,* the intermingling of energy fields that is characteristic of empathy, compassion, and the group mind. Bonding in communities is a result of the social brain. Bonding is therapeutic; it cultivates a sense of integrated wholeness, which enhances healing (https://www.frontiersin.org/articles/10.3389/fpsyg.2018.02584/full).

Leaps in consciousness are marked by bursts of neuroplasticity and synaptic growth in the brain that measure as increased electromagnetic energy and frequencies of light.

The brain lights up when we integrate new information, feel inspiration, play a musical instrument, learn a foreign language, problem solve, or handle new tasks. Physical exercises that build coordination also light up the brain, as do positive feelings and creative thoughts. This heightened brain activity indicates neurogenesis and synaptic growth. Brain studies on musicians have shown that training hand and finger sensitivity expands the creative capacity of the brain, as well as the ways in which we learn. Focused touch floods the nervous system with new connections that run between the fingers and the brain—new brain mapping and expanded perception. Consciousness is transformed any time brain mapping is changed, and in the case of learning, consciousness expands.

I suspect that my own brain mapping has been positively crafted by the choices I've made in life, and I am grateful. Yoga asana practice since 1971 has given me highly sensitized perceptual skills and body intuition, and these ways of knowing enhance my work. My hands have been trained by thirty years of practicing bodywork and massage. I can sense subtle layers of body tissue, temperature variances, nerve disturbances, fear, struggle, resistance, and release. My hands get hot when I work, and transmit healing power too. The potential for brain evolution is available to us all. How we each express it will be unique to us.

It's been shown that mentally rehearsing on a musical instrument is as effective as actually playing it, creating a learned memory and lighting up all the same brain regions in all the same ways as actually playing. Clearly, focus evolves the brain into a creative force.

Neuroplasticity occurs when we imprint new patterns of thinking and behavior through repetition. Connectivity lights up the brain. The more light in the brain, the higher and more resonant our vibrational frequency and the faster we heal.

We acquire new habits by practice. What if we were to replace the brain circuits that cause us injury and pain with habits that nurture and build strength? The brain is very practical: it learns quickly what to save and regularly prunes out what we no longer use. Repetitive thoughts and habits show up in the brain's map of active circuits. Conscious choice is the path to evolutionary neuroplasticity in the brain. This profound power belongs to each one of us who chooses to claim it.

What we do every day influences us more than what we do every now and then. Like any skill, meditation, breathing, and awareness are practices to integrate into our lives.

Practices for Daily Life

Simple awareness practice: Generate self-love and improve self-esteem.

1. **Notice every time you put yourself down or minimize an accomplishment.** This blocks your potential and dims your faith.

2. **Play sleuth with self-sabotage. Turn it around on the spot.** Mentally cross out and cancel any negative statements you make about yourself inside your own head. Say something affirmative instead.
3. **Continue for thirty days.**

Positive emotions carry more light than sadness and self-blame. These practices reshape the brain and generate light and life force. They are simple to do anytime and anywhere. Minimal effort and privacy are required to eavesdrop on our own thoughts.

As inner light expands, so does possibility. Hope and inspiration return, adding momentum to our progress. We finally glimpse—and step into—our true soul power.

How Trauma Keeps Us Stuck

I recently asked a group I was speaking to this question: "What really causes pain and disease?" They gave many brilliant answers, which was a living testimony to how far we have come in knowledge and awareness. However, all their responses missed the one key point: *trauma.*

Strong shocks activate the survival brain and, if not processed, can persist subconsciously, limiting our relationships, health, and beliefs.

Traumas form our unconscious attitudes about safety, support, and what we deserve and can expect from the world. Traumas, whether physical or emotional, thrust the brain and nervous system into fear, anxiety, and withdrawal. These subconscious patterns remain lodged in the body. In my experience, unresolved trauma is an underlying factor in pain and degeneration and is the reason many people never heal.

Early childhood traumas can have lasting impact on health.

Because the prefrontal cortex develops as we mature, babies lack cognitive skills. Babies can't debrief themselves or rationalize away unfounded fears. Their emotions and instincts form their initial perceptions and beliefs about life. Without the *body memory* of receiving support in early life, babies become developmentally stunted adults wired to operate in survival mode: fight, flight, or freeze. When connectivity is shut down at this early age, the social brain doesn't develop, and the emotional landscape is marked by anxiety, lack of bonding, and lack of trust. Bringing panic down in the body, the nervous system, and the brain (sympathetic down-regulation) is where real healing starts, at any age.

The process of autonomic nervous system regulation must be somatic (body-based).

Talk therapy alone can't reach it. Preverbal memories are unconsciously buried in the body, from where they direct our lives "to keep us safe." If these early traumas are not addressed at the body level, injuries and traumas will continue to pile on top of them throughout life; then we lose the possibility for resilience that is fundamental to survival and growth.

Somatic therapies like yoga and bodywork help the body and consciousness heal trauma and pain.

Recently, psychiatrist Bessel Vanderkolk introduced groundbreaking research regarding our unconscious body memories of trauma and the importance of somatic therapies for healing. He wasn't the first human ever to claim this, but he was the first medical psychiatrist to provide the indisputable trauma therapy research our world needed to recognize and resolve these unseen causes of physical pain and mental illness.

Habitual negativity, reactivity, and depression may be defensive survival mechanisms that stem from early childhood trauma.

The same holds true for repeated accidents and relationship conflicts; unconscious behavior patterns evolve from our repressed trauma and abuse. The body remembers everything. Our cells, fluids, and tissue layers carry the tales. Danger may be kept alive as an energy within us by ancestral survival strategies and unconscious beliefs. Ancestral trauma leaves its epigenetic mark on the whole family line. Our brains and nervous systems are supercomputers programmed to patrol for danger and keep us alive, and what we believe becomes what we see.

Yogis, shamans, and mystics didn't need scientific proof to benefit from the wisdom of interconnectedness. They *felt* it.

Our culture tends to place no value on direct experience. We bypass interconnection, and demand "scientific proof" for everything. To the mystic, direct experience – which is available to us through self-reflection and spiritual practice - is the teacher and guide. To end the chaos of our times, we will need to make this leap of faith ourselves and go within. We've waited centuries for science to validate mysticism, and now that it has, we have even more reasons to do this work. Spirituality is a mass movement today, and science gives it ground and backing and big winds under its wings.

The holistic quest for wellness today leads directly into the great mystery and the realm between spirit and matter. By intimately embracing the tapestry of life within us—its complexity and its wonder—we touch the universal energies that govern creation as a whole.

Neuroscience and the Brain

> In the absence of connection, vital brain circuits pull back and shrivel, rendering us emotionally and spiritually bereft. The brain shrinks with trauma and shock. This makes us more prone to feel disconnected and depressed. It also interrupts learning, movement, and relationships. Brain cells regenerate if we give them a chance!
>
> —Y. Pritam Hari

Isolation and Brain Shrinkage

Isolation is rampant in our culture, and it makes us physically and mentally ill. We get desynchronized when we feel cut off.

Brain waves project electromagnetic fields and announce our presence to each other long before we arrive. Our individual and collective electromagnetic fields are forming the environment right now! In isolation, depression, and illness, the field becomes disorganized and withdraws, perpetuating discordance. Healthy brains, however, produce coherent waves and vibrant electromagnetic fields that uplift and heal.

When synaptic connections in the brain die off, we lose life force.

The body becomes disturbed and confused, and we experience anxiety, depression, pain, and disease. *Modern medicine tends not to pay attention to this at all.* If baby chimps and rabbits are isolated and not held, they lose interest in life, withdraw, and die. Ducks and geese who lose a mate usually perish quickly themselves. So do many widowed spouses who were married for fifty or sixty years. Trauma, head injuries, and pharmaceuticals are silent, insidious causes of brain degeneration and decay. Likewise, connection, social support, and brain therapies all address the cycle of trauma, pain, isolation, and brain shrinkage that is causing so much of our pain.

Connectivity and Body Healing

Connectivity is clearly signaled and transmitted through touch.

Touch receptors on our skin feed endorphins to the brain and body, and convey to us the sense that we *belong*. New synaptic connections start to sprout right away.

Yet too many people in our culture are rarely, if ever, touched. This disconnection and isolation are great sources of failing immunity, depression, and suicide.

Sadvi Saraswati and Bruce Lipton cite studies showing that people who live in spiritual community with loving relationships have enhanced immune function, better attitudes, and zero percent relapse of cancer, while the general populace leans the other way.

In this Internet age, connection is a strictly mental phenomenon, and this adversely affects our cell metabolism and relationships.

Research notes a culture-wide breakdown in our ability to communicate face to face now that all our relationships are virtual. Other studies show that our attention spans are now frightfully short (a few seconds).

Forbes had this to say: "At no other point in history have we had access to such a broad audience right at our fingertips, which is a great thing for brands to build on. Yet, this platform sometimes makes us overlook the quality of relationships versus the quantity of how many we have … With how in-tune our world is with digital, it's time to start making our interactions more authentic."

Here's that article: https://www.forbes.com/sites/ajagrawal/2017/05/04/millennials-are-struggling-with-face-to-face-communication-heres-why/#54ebce4e26e8.

Says Marketing CEO Kyle Reyes, "The more I interact with millennials—whether I'm interviewing them, overseeing internships or giving speeches to them—the more I see an entire generation that doesn't know how to communicate." And according to Business Insider, "By 2020, Millennials will spend most of their energy sharing short social messages, being entertained, and being distracted away from deep engagement with people and knowledge." They'll lack "deep-thinking capabilities" and "face-to-face social skills" (https://www.businessinsider.com/millennials-are-losing-social-skills-2012-3).

Without quality time in person, and real touch, we are training our brains to sever connectivity to the heart, and this does not bode well for our heath, happiness, or evolution as a species. Real relationships are vital. They keep the heart and soul alive.

Intuition and healing are matters of the heart.

We're on the verge of *losing touch* with everything that makes life real. But it's not too late. We only need to slow down and get reconnected.

Still, there's a lot of atmospheric interference from the global reach of the Internet, so it's essential to take time away from that environment and visit natural settings. Electromagnetic smog and atmospheric radiation cause us extreme physiological stress and have been clearly linked to cancers and tumors, but that information is seriously suppressed. Furthermore, cellular damage is amplified by living in a culture of constant overstimulation, nervous anxiety, and pressure to do more and more.

Stress of any kind activates the survival brain. In short bursts, stress expands neural capacity (positive neurogenesis), but in excess, it destroys brain and nerve tissue, enzymes, and hormones. Chronic stress also burns out the adrenals, especially when the excess energy from stress hormones is not spent or diffused. We need exercise to balance out, but people who are too busy or living in pain rarely get enough; for them, it's just too hard. Still, even those with disabilities can practice breathwork, mudras, singing and chanting to stimulate their organs and meditation to train their minds.

Degenerative disorders and adrenal fatigue are epidemic in our world right now.

Drugs won't fix this; we have to address the root causes in order to heal. Four vital keys to balance are physical activity, expressing our creativity, detoxification, and technology fasts. Time away from the constant bombardment of radioactive frequencies gives our brains a chance to heal and reboot. Without breaks, cellular breakdown eventually goes beyond what we can repair. Our bodies stagnate without breaks.

We may not realize that postural imbalances create patterns of internal tension and collapse, which damage muscles, organs, and nerve transmission. Progressive degeneration is a direct effect.

Imbalance on any level sooner or later shows up in body structure. Imagine the posture of heartache, a bellyache, or depression. The body collapses in on itself; organ systems are compromised and begin to shut down. Consider also the posture and movement of someone with a twisted ankle, shoulder injury, or back pain. Very likely, the person leans to one side and limps or locks the injured arm down against the ribs. Asymmetry signals danger to the nervous system. Adaptive compensations in posture and movement perpetuate chronic compression and increase physical strain and limitation.

If we knew and trusted our bodies, we could repair injuries and damage for ourselves at the start. But once symptoms become chronic, we will benefit from professional help. The best solution for chronic tension is skilled touch. Bodywork and massage have an infinite array of techniques for assessing and treating the core of most pain: *postural and emotional stress.* Physical realignment work and postural symmetry strengthen bone structure and emotional resilience. *It's all stored within.*

Movement practices improve metabolism, emotional balance, and fluid exchange. Walking, deep breathing, and other forms of exercise pump the blood and lymph, which improves our immunity and detoxifies our organs. Yoga postures help clear the organs directly, especially when the focus is on alignment and breath. Structural yoga creates healthy alignment that stabilizes the body and mind.

Sleep

Sleep heals the brain. Sleep is a vital key to healing and self-repair.

Sleep activates ***glial cells,*** the brain cells involved in repair and regeneration, in clearing toxins and metabolic wastes, and in producing the ***myelin sheath*** that coats our nerves.

Glia are highly active during deep REM sleep.

Rest and sleep are essential for nervous system self-regulation and brain repair. Chronic hyperstimulation in the absence of sufficient deep sleep snaps brain connections and inhibits the brain repair that only happens at night. Prolonged sleep deprivation leads to brain inflammation, nerve shrinkage, and psychological trauma, because the glial cells can't do their repair work. During sleep, the brain goes into healing mode. Deep sleep increases circulation around the brain, reducing pain, agitation, inflammation, panic, and fear. **Glial brain cells make up 90 percent of the brain's content, and half of its weight.**

This brain's system of cleanup, renewal, and repair functions overnight in absolute darkness, during REM sleep. But considering our entire culture is chronically overstimulated and sleep deprived, this precious self-healing system doesn't have sufficient time to turn on and go to work; and sometimes it malfunctions by pruning out healthy cells instead of damaged ones.

Sleep disorders and degenerative disease are on the rise, while our glial system is being destroyed by toxic buildups of metabolites, chemicals that cross the blood-brain barrier, and heavy metals that bind the calcium signaling that is supposed to turn the glia on. Glia are also damaged by poor sleep hygiene—such as when tech devices or electrical equipment run 24/7 in the same room.

Another recently recognized fact is that impact injuries, especially to the head, can damage or even destroy the glial brain.

It's easy to miss the connection. With brain and nervous system injury, symptoms can appear much later, and the damage is cumulative over time. Head injuries reshape the brain, damage circuits, and disrupt the body's electromagnetic field. It's a vicious cycle too. Being stuck in a state of being overwhelmed by the fight-flight-freeze response creates residual anxiety, fear, and pain.

Enlightenment and Our Sacred Fluids

It's been said that we are moving beyond the power of manifestation and into the law of radiance. This is to be our next quantum leap.

Fluids circulating in the body are sacred pathways for radiance—for the light. *The body is 78 percent water.* Living cells produce electricity and magnetism, and when nerve impulses travel through our fluid-plasma landscape within, they emit sparks.

Nerves transmit instant memos through our fascia. During these bioelectric exchanges, fluids and fascia in the body spark with light. Neuroscientists have done brain scans and EEGs, measuring the brain frequencies emitted by monks and *rinpoches* in deep meditation. Dr. Joe Dispenza, author of *Becoming Supernatural,* has done brain scans of lay people in his week-long meditation retreats to document brain waves and structural changes in their brains. In all cases, focused meditation practices vastly **increased neuroplastic brain changes and luminescence in the cells.** Along with scans of vibrant colors and patterns in the meditators' brains, their electromagnetic biofields, or auras, radiated measurable light. As this body of light grows, it mingles and merges with surrounding light frequencies, adding its potency, frequency, and influence to the whole.

Thich Nhat Hanh refers to our interconnectedness as "interbeing." We are literally one interconnected fluid organism, one pulsing field of light.

Physics named this intermingling of energy fields *entanglement.* Yogis call it *Indra's net.*

Across the board, the story is exactly the same. Nothing exists in isolation. Everything is interconnected. *All is one.* In this interconnected and interrelated universe, everything affects everything else, and all possibilities coexist.

I am so excited by these resources that I am sharing the links right away, instead of in the list at the end of the book. These images of Indra's net are exactly what I saw in visions as a child and see in meditation now!

https://www.scienceandnonduality.com/the-indras-net/

https://www.uua.org/re/tapestry/youth/bridges/workshop7/indra

Within our genetic code is the potential for self-healing and regeneration, just waiting for consciousness to bring it to life.

Before Western culture made it a fitness routine at the gym, the original purpose of yoga was human evolution. Yoga is a time-tested science of human potential, based on meditation, focus, and intention. It takes patience and humility to go within, flush the mental and emotional sludge, and *wake up*—and to revive our relationship with our true selves.

Although *stretching* is a beneficial side effect of yoga, it's really about mastering our minds for creativity, healing, and service to the times. With just a little willingness, we can recover our innate superpowers and reconnect to the source of life.

Epigenetics **is the new science of DNA.**

Through decades of research on stem cells, biologist Bruce Lipton found that evolution is programmed by the environment of the cells, *not* the genes themselves. Lipton says that genes are blueprints, turned on and off by our attitudes and beliefs. Thoughts and beliefs create our biochemistry, and DNA responds to *all of this*—just as cells in a petri dish respond to their chemical culture.

This is a crucial starting point for holistic healing today.

Healing, like evolution, is nonmaterial, nonmechanical, and nonlocal. *It's energetic.* Healing happens through connection—with our bodies and emotions, nature and spirit, each other, and our own personal relationship with faith, trust, and the unknown. In the scope of infinity, anything is possible. If we open up healthy flow in the body, light is expressed in the fluid tapestry of our cells. If not, we remain stuck in struggle and old patterns.

Fluids must flow in order for life to flourish. We are mentally and physically flexible when our fluids are circulating. Mental and physical rigidity limits the body's ability to transmit nerve energy and life force. This dims our potential and our ability to feel faith, trust, and connection and to regulate our bodies for happiness and health. But evolution is a two-way slide; we always have choice. We are not victims of fate. Our consciousness will determine the final acts of this play.

The Crisis of Spiritual Breakthrough

The human journey includes the possibility for expanded states of consciousness where things seem "larger than life."

In truth, spiritual breakthroughs are both exalting and extreme. They aren't always disruptive, but since they *can* be, this conversation must be had before we proceed. The market dilutes and sensationalizes everything so that it appeals to the modern mind, which diminishes its depth and value but makes it easy to sell. For example, in magazines, everyone smiles idyllically while meditating, which is a shallow and inaccurate depiction of spiritual practice. There's more to all of this than meets the eye.

In our culture, sudden spiritual breakthroughs are usually diagnosed as mental illness and and completely shut down with antipsychotic drugs. This level of insensitivity during such a vulnerable and potent time actually *can* lead to mental breakdowns, as the full force of creation retreats back into the human psyche and body tissues, unexpressed. Once evolutionary energy awakens, it's way too big to hold inside, and the nervous system can be overwhelmed by suppression, sudden surges, and uninformed psychiatric care. The brain is in a delicate and extreme state of flux, and the energy of creation cannot be restricted or controlled. It can, however, be channeled toward our higher purpose through yoga and other forms of spiritual practice.

To the outer world in modern times, people undergoing spiritual breakthroughs may appear to be manic, psychotic, or insane. The individuals themselves may feel crazed. But things are not always as they appear. There are two sides to every coin.

Our souls long to grow. Spiritual breakthrough is a very sacred thing.

Indigenous peoples of all cultures throughout time were mystically aligned in reverent relationship with the forces and cycles of nature and the stars. Their lives were lived in profound union with Source, Spirit, the One. Knowing we are held in the lap of something greater nurtures the human heart. This blesses us with a sense of belonging, comfort, and peace. Then we *naturally* turn to offer ourselves back to the earth and all her creatures. Yet how far we seem to have strayed from honoring relationships with each other, nature, and spirit. Connectivity is vital to life.

Devotional rituals which invoke the vibrational state of connection and oneness can collectively be called *prayer*.

Prayer is a feeling of deep gratitude for the grace of life. Prayer is also a statement of our desires, and a powerful force field that influences situations and environments. When we are inwardly connected, brain signals and mental processes are reorganized. Emotions are elevated, and synchronicities occur with greater regularity. Prayer becomes affirmative and absolute, and the universe responds. At times in the process of spiritual breakthrough, however, the electromagnetic energies in the brain and nerves are overamplified, and equilibrium is disturbed.

Transpersonal psychiatrist Stan Grof coined the term **spiritual emergence** as an accepted psychiatric diagnosis, completely apart from mental illness. He recognized the need to help patients integrate this sacred soul awakening, and he created a breathwork system to accomplish this without drugs. Breath is the therapeutic bridge to unconscious gripping and fear, and Grof was familiar with its potent natural healing effects. Grof defined *spiritual emergence* as "the movement of an individual to a more expanded way of being that involves enhanced emotional and psychosomatic health, greater freedom of personal choices, and a sense of deeper connection with other people, nature, and the cosmos. An important part of this development is an increasing awareness of the spiritual dimension in one's life and in the universal scheme of things."

Transpersonal psychologist Diana Raab, PhD, added this: "Spiritual emergency … typically is triggered by a physical or emotional life-enhancing or awe-inspiring experience. It may also be triggered by a lack of sleep, or matters related to childbirth, miscarriage, or abortion. Extreme sexual experiences can also result in a spiritual emergency. Sometimes the trigger may be connected to a deep spiritual practice or meditation. Another interesting fact is that often those experiencing spiritual emergencies seem to seek self-expression in the arts through painting, music, or writing—all languages of the soul. Spiritual emergencies may be classified as peak experiences, past-life experiences, channeling with spirit guides, Kundalini experiences, dark and night possessions, near-death experiences, UFO encounters, or drug and alcohol addictions."

As we see, everyday life experiences provide ample opportunities for this sort of breakthrough to occur, and it challenges and changes us.

Whether from spiritual practice and initiation or due to embodied trauma and shock, activation comes suddenly. *Kundalini*—spiritual force—is a powerful burst of grace. But because so many neural circuits are all activated at once, awakening comes on strong, and it can be overwhelming. Historically, mystics have repeatedly ridden the delicate and difficult continuum between ecstasy and the *dark night of the soul*. Spiritual literature is full of this. To our detriment in modern times, this awakening can be labeled by psychiatry as psychosis.

In quantum activation, the brain and nervous system get amped up quickly, and the vast pressure differentials inside us can jolt our most sensitive organs, the brain and the heart.

One analogy would be a baby being born by C-section; another is a diver surfacing from the depths too fast. These are rapid barometric pressure changes, and *a period of regulation must follow.* When spiritual emergence is fast and dramatic, and there is no available guidance or support, it becomes a crisis—a ***spiritual emergency.***

A **spiritual emergency** involves immense psychological struggle and transformation of one's entire being. Transpersonal psychologist Paul Levy says, "A spiritual awakening is almost always precipitated by a severe emotional or spiritual crisis; *it oftentimes organically grows out of unresolved abuse issues from childhood*—this was certainly true in my case. In a fully-flowered spiritual emergence, you magically discover how *to transmute these symptoms and wounds into the blessings that they are.*"

Mind-body medicine, holistic healing, and consciousness studies offer this same conclusion: by facing and healing our emotional wounds, we find the true gifts and strengths within us that we can share.

Levy's article is included here because his viewpoint is extremely helpful for someone in the midst of spiritual crisis. As individuals and cultures, we are on the verge of breaking through—and when we recognize this all around us, or go through it ourselves, the voice of experience is a rope to grab at when we reach the precipice's edge.

https://www.awakeninthedream.com/articles/spiritual-emergence

When the influx of Kundalini energy is met consciously with care, a heightened baseline for the spiritual nervous system is set. We become open channels for the power of the universe flowing through us as life, and our radiance becomes visible, palpable, and real.

Quantum Activation, Kundalini, and Pebbles on the Path

Quantum activation is the moment of becoming suddenly and vibrantly awake. In this exalted, superconscious state of being, anything is possible.

We are tuned in, all pistons firing; the game is on. The universal energy existing in the quantum field vibrates at unimaginably high frequencies, far exceeding those of the dense material world. Creation dances itself to life each moment, in extraordinary ways. This is the theme of mystic poetry from all spiritual traditions, and of the shaman's song. In the quantum field, which is the realm of consciousness beyond time, space, and separation, we cease to be limited by thoughts, doubts, or cultural expectations.

The quantum field is the divine frequency of harmony, love, and bliss. It's the totality of space from which we all came and to which we all return. The quantum field is the womb of all creation. It's the infinite sea of energy containing all that is.

Quantum activation is a flash of consciousness that weaves us fully and indisputably into the whole, evoking epiphanies for the soul.

Humans have always sought connection to something greater and pursued that connection through ritual, worship, meditation, and prayer. Spiritual traditions build inner light by activating the power of the quantum field. Divine union is our true nature. But the industrial age courted human intellect instead and dismissed the human soul, so our ancestors began to lose their way. Today, generations later, many of us remain disconnected from the true source of life. This pivotal juncture in time is the choice point for our future as a species. Studies show that group consciousness has the power to influence global events and personal health. Quantum physics describes the universe as a vast field of interactive intelligence containing all life. The seeds of quantum activation have been planted for us. Human potential is limitless in the quantum field.

Science has crossed the threshold into the sacred, and we are being shuttled back to our spiritual roots. We can supercharge our physiology through deep meditation and rituals that anchor light. Consciousness is infinitely expansive; we discover this by going within. Spiritual practice is the portal. The world is calling, and the time is *now*.

Mystics believe the pineal and pituitary glands receive and transmit the light of higher consciousness.

The pineal gland contains microcrystalline particles that process and reflect light, which the pituitary area amplifies. Tiny little calcite crystals in the pineal gland produce **luminescense,** a type of **light** without heat. This may explain why, in yoga, the pineal and pituitary glands comprise the third eye center, *ajna chakra*. In his book *Treatise of Man,* mathematician-philosopher Rene Descartes wrote of the pineal, "This gland is the principle seat of the soul, and the place in which all thoughts are formed." Biologically, the pineal gland controls sleep-wake cycles and other hypothalamic functions like hormone balance, reproduction, and mood. Meditating in the dark before dawn increases pineal activity and melatonin production, which regulates overall health. Yogis intuitively knew this. Brain activation in the early morning creates hormonal cascades and enhances our inner vision and knowing.

Says the Bible: **"If therefore thine eye be single, thy whole body shall be full of light"** (Matthew, 6:22, KJV).

Our bodies are, in so many ways, potentially full of light. We nurture this divine capacity by making smart choices. Chemicals like chlorine, fluoride, and bromide calcify the pineal and pituitary glands, disrupting hormone production, sleep, intuition, and immune function and thus, dulling our inner light. But living systems are capable of **regeneration.** The pineal and pituitary glands can be revived through detoxification, meditation, high-quality brain supplements and foods, and bodywork that activates brain fluid flow (blood, lymph, cerebrospinal, and interstitial fluids). Detoxification includes consciously eliminating potential toxins as well as cleansing their accumulation.

In addition to fostering brain repair, fluid circulation helps soften restrictions and realign the body from within. Alignment opens pathways for circulation, chakra luminescence, and self-repair. Energy that moves through the spinal cord (or chakra system) carries evolutionary force. As mentioned previously, our bodies have a natural instinct to survive, and the pressures we face today are forcing us to adapt and evolve. This dynamic has its own momentum, influenced by our choices but not subject to our control. Evolutionary transformation is already in process.

Kundalini is awakening across the planet now. But she doesn't make an appointment and can take over our lives in a flash.

As more people invest themselves in spiritual practices like meditation and prayer, planetary evolution surges, and the power of self-healing and group consciousness increases. Kundalini energy overhauls and reorganizes our body structures, emotions, and life force. Our nervous systems are upgraded to higher frequencies of light. We are changing and evolving so fast that equilibrium is challenging. Moments of balance ebb and flow. Much like when we clean out a closet, renovate rooms, or paint the walls, the house could be messy for a while. It's best to just be patient and attentive and try to sweep up at the end of the day.

Evolutionary upgrades challenge and empower us to thrive.

Crisis sparks evolution and spiritual growth. The healing path is a spiritual path. Pandora's box seems to be cracking open across the planet, pushing all our known limits. Between internal pressures and outer circumstances, we may feel deranged, as if we are swinging between extremes. The traumas that have shaped our psyches have shut parts of us down, and these parts may be seeking resolution now. It's all just energy in motion, but it until it settles, it can be quite intense. What if we knew we were on the verge of personal breakthrough? Wouldn't the difficulty seem far less?

At this rich and vulnerable moment, meditation and self-care are vital to anchoring consciousness in the present moment despite the groundlessness that we feel. Physical activity metabolizes stress hormones. When we feel strong emotions in the absence of immediate threat, breathwork and movement will defuse the charge. Walk, dance, play sports, do yoga, or get a massage. Self-care includes receiving support through bodywork, counseling, and spiritual mentorship.

During times of upheaval, holistic therapies help ground us in our bodies and stabilize our emotions. The ego may resist needing support, but this is an unproductive pattern, which conscious awareness can change. Let's recall that isolation shrinks the brain, while connectivity spawns synaptic growth—new nerve pathways and new possibilities. Trust and connection also develop heart intelligence and coherence. Through heart resonance we silently invite the whisper of body wisdom to guide and direct our healing, relationships, creative self-expression, and evolutionary growth.

Reexamining Trauma and Spiritual Growth

Spiritual maturity is a lifelong process of initiation. Growth isn't always comfortable, linear, or smooth.

Meeting our inner obstacles and limitations, we hit bumps in the road. Kundalini brings up powerful emotions. Kundalini may surge spontaneously by divine grace, with no obvious precursor. But usually we find a cellular memory surfacing for release—a body memory. Buried trauma is toxic to the body and mind, increasing anxiety, agitation, and fear. This defies evolution, so the spirit casts it off.

Fear stays alive in the nervous system, cemented into our body tissues by *subconscious* beliefs from the past.

Under extreme stress, the body struggles and, to keep functioning, pushes the pain ever deeper inside. At a certain point, these energies can no longer be contained; they overwhelm the nervous system, and breakdown occurs. Medical doctors prescribe antipsychotic drugs, which drive the pain deeper into the body. Without somatic (body-based) forms of release, internal strain progresses to panic, pain, insomnia, metabolic disorders, and eventually disease. We need healing practices to balance our bodies and emotions. Bodywork and yoga enhance the flow of life force. Physical and energetic alignment connect us into the flow of life. Once we understand the process consciously, the seeming crisis of spiritual activation can be less intense.

The nervous system is highly activated by trauma, chronic pain, and Kundalini, yet each requires a different response from us.

Excitement and agitation run the same circuitry in the brain: high sympathetic nervous system activity—a lot of energy! When quick, strong bursts of nerve energy spark, we feel this excess energy in diverse ways, from being anxious and restless to inspired. These sudden evolutionary influxes catapult overall energy so much that we may appear manic to the outer eye. We may be mentally disorganized. *It's not business as usual, for sure.*

The brain and nervous system invest energy to keep us safe.

There are two branches to the nervous system: one that speeds us up into fight-flight-freeze mode (sympathetic), and one that slows us down to rest, relax, and heal (parasympathetic). Together, they are known as the *autonomic nervous system* (ANS). Biologically, these complementary systems should balance each other like yang and yin to create harmony in our bodies, minds, and lives. Modern society, however, is chronically stressed, cortisol driven, and operating on high alert. As long as the survival brain is locked in the fight-flight-freeze response, the body is unable to relax or heal. *Healing begins when the parasympathetic nervous system wakes up.* Manual therapies, spiritual practices, and self-care serve this purpose.

Movement defuses the charge of anxiety, restlessness, and fear. We must do something physical.

Until we *physically* discharge trauma from the body, its influence remains in the body tissue, patterning our reactions and responses to life. Talk therapy alone can't access these deeper parts of the survival brain or reason with the volcanic force of evolution surging through. This *quantum power* rising within us needs to be met, grounded, and channeled toward its higher purpose—evolution. The most practical actions for accomplishing this are bodywork, counseling, and somatic practices like yoga, breathwork, or tai chi. This course of care gradually rewires the brain and nervous system for health, bonding, and connection. Transformation inevitably requires that old patterns break down to make way for new configurations. We die to our old selves to birth the new. In the process of this transmutation, we will feel groundless and fragmented for a while. It can be challenging, and we may at times feel drastically shaken off course.

Mythology is filled with dramatically colorful tales about the hero's journey, the human odyssey seen through the lens of the spiritual eye. Gardens go fallow in winter, and fresh, green leaves emerge in the spring. In the wake of wildfires, new shoots pop up. In the same way, Kundalini activation is a breakthrough of spirit, a blooming spring and summer season for the soul, where heroic voltage is generated in the brain.

Dissolution precedes self-renewal.

The Chinese use the same word for *crisis* and *opportunity*. As we pass through the cosmic birth canal, evolving into ourselves, every last vestige of who we once were is peeled away. Ego surrenders to heart and soul. The labor contractions can be dynamic and fierce. It's not at all like airbrushed photos in yoga and meditation magazines where everyone wears idyllic smiles.

Self-transformation is a remarkable opportunity for breakthrough, equal to the challenge it presents. During this transition, we need safe places and times to fall apart. We need healers, friends, family, and community sensitive enough to hold space for profound emotional and spiritual opening. There will be times when silence and solitude are called for to soothe the raging storms inside, but with bodywork, self-care, community, and spiritual support, we uproot the past and expand into the radiance produced by our own cells. It's a miraculous gift to receive steady, focused therapeutic support and in the process, wake up on the bright side of a rough and terrifying wave.

We can change virtually anything about ourselves.

Neurogenesis—the birth of new brain and nerve cells—is a blueprint programmed in our DNA. Feeling hope, compassion, inspiration, and positivity—*and* learning new things—heals and integrates the brain.

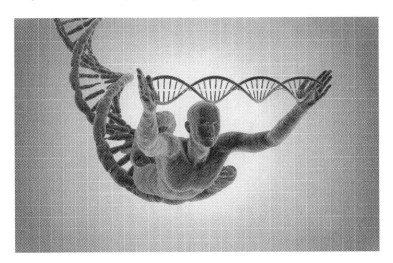

Our brains neuroplasticize—reconfigure—whenever we learn anything new, for better or for worse. With devoted training and practice, we can skillfully steer our troubling inner tides. People suffer needlessly in their bodies by *not* knowing how to find and awaken their self-healing powers within. When we examine our beliefs and edit the thoughts and information we allow in, our brains sprout new synapses that spread like fireworks spraying across the night sky, and we gain access to our natural potential for self-repair.

All the tools for self-healing and radiance are waiting inside us. Consciousness is the doorway to awakening. Presence and compassion are the keys.

SECTION 5

Sensitivity Syndromes through the Eyes of Compassion

Our Shared Common Threads

We are essentially the same in many ways. The suffering we undergo as humans has a common thread in the body*: it's* ***neurological.***

The brain and nerves are physical conduits for life force here on earth, through which our consciousness expresses itself. Many people alive today have extremely sensitive nervous systems and are chronically desynchronized by any combination of factors: chemical and environmental toxins, EMF radiation, constant noise and overstimulation, unrelenting pain, sleeplessness, or unresolved traumas walled off inside.

The more we learn, the more we recognize that our diverse symptoms and diagnoses all in some way involve the nervous system and the brain. Everything we experience puts out electrical signals. This could actually simplify assessment and treatment for our suffering patients and clients.

For example, in my work with complex pain and mysterious clusters of symptoms, clients frequently ask how I find "the right place." Old traumas, fears, and chemicals stay compartmentalized in the body tissue, and the toxic buildup disturbs the nerves. Nerve disturbances show up to my hands as sensations of static electricity that project out like barriers beyond the surface of the client's skin. In this way, the body cautiously guides us straight to the core issue and the resolution it desires. The static is almost always an unconscious reaction to a fearful body memory or a toxic chemical or environmental allergen assaulting the brain. Healthy tissue does not put out static; it feels neutral and smooth.

Every therapist has his or her own way of perceiving, which, although informed by knowledge and study, seems directed by an intuitive *body sense*. For me, the feeling of static electricity or pronounced heat emanating from their tissues draws my hands. I see and feel static, and I sense temperature differentials around the vortex or core of the complaint—which is often not where they feel their tension and pain. *Their natural physiological processes communicate with me.* The nervous system welcomes contact—direct or indirect—when it senses our compassionate intention to assist its healing and relieve strain.

Everything's neurological, and that can't be said that enough.

All forms of consciousness express self-healing and contain the potential energy to create and sustain life. Here on earth, consciousness expresses itself through the central nervous system, the electromagnetic circuitry embedded within our human flesh. The universe seems to have a nervous system too, an intelligence—or consciousness—that is interwoven with everything it contains, which includes us. Whether animal, vegetal, or universal, consciousness naturally seeks balance and order. Atomic, subatomic, and celestial processes undergo electromagnetic interactions and establish self-regulating fields. The entire continuum of the cosmos, which science calls the *quantum field,* rewires itself and self-regulates. When disturbed, *it heals itself.* We can too, but the challenges and obstacles seem great. Bodywork is a direct means of reestablishing coherence, connection, and regulation, and of harmonizing the human nervous system with the universal intelligence of the quantum field for evolution and self-healing.

Sensitivity Syndromes and Degenerative Disease

Neurological, degenerative, and autoimmune disorders are on the rise. These conditions are related. All cause hypersensitivity in the nervous system and progressive declines in brain health.

The following disorders are dubbed ***central sensitivity syndromes*** because they involve and strongly affect the central nervous system (the brain and spinal cord). I prefer the term ***sensitivity syndromes*** myself, because we become hypersensitive when our nerves are stripped raw, whether by prolonged stress, injury, trauma, or disease.

Two familiar sensitivity syndromes are fibromyalgia syndrome (FMS) and chronic fatigue syndrome (CFS). Recently, traumas and abuses from early life—known as adverse childhood experiences (ACEs)—have also been linked to brain and nerve degeneration and lifelong declines in physical, emotional, and mental health.

Patient histories of FMS, CFS, and ACEs, when reviewed, often show past trauma, neglect, and repeated disappointments in life. Emotional trauma has the same capacity as the physical trauma of head injuries to damage and shrink the brain. With FMS, CFS, and ACEs, there might also have been a virulent childhood illness, bacterial infection, or virus that left its scars and restrictions inside. The active infection may be long gone, but brain and nerve inflammation remain, worsening slowly over time. Circulation is blocked by both the original and residual inflammations, and this injures nerves so the brain and body remain unable to self-heal. Because sensitivity syndromes are invisible, mysterious, and disabling, residual PTSD, shame, and social withdrawal may be factors as well.

Two more classes of neurological conditions have now been named: Ehlers-Danlos syndrome (EDS) and hypermobility disorders (HMD). EDS and HMD remain the least known, recognized, or understood among sensitivity syndromes. For these people, excess flexibility is pathological, and they are chronically injured because their tendons don't hold their bones in place. With their bodies in danger of destabilizing all the time, their nerves remain on high alert.

In all of these conditions, insomnia is common. Meanwhile, we know that REM sleep is essential for wellness and healing. Deep sleep heals and regenerates the body and the brain. Glial cell activation—the brain's marching army of cleanup and repair—and cerebrospinal fluid drainage and flow increase at night, all working in tandem to heal and restore.

> Turn the waters of life loose at the brain, remove all hindrances and the work will be done, and give us the eternal legacy, longevity.

> —A. T. Still, MD, DO, *Philosophy of Osteopathy*

The brain and body can't access self-repair without restful sleep. This cycle is vicious in our culture, especially for those on the sensitivity spectrum. With central sensitivity syndromes, we often find fascial strains and scarring somewhere in the cranial membrane system surrounding the brain. Strains, scarring, and inflammation all limit fluid perfusion (circulation through and around the brain tissue). As mentioned earlier, in the absence of healthy fluid flow, cell metabolism gradually shuts down. Like a polluted lake, the brain matrix slowly stagnates, and progressive diseases take hold. As symptoms worsen, chronic depletion, depression, anxiety, and personality changes result. Manual therapies like bodywork, osteopathy, chiropractic, and acupuncture have immense potential to turn these symptoms and epidemics around because they move stagnant energy and help the nervous system rest and reset.

Craniosacral and brain-lymph therapies are rooted in osteopathy—a gentle, precise manual therapy system that addresses membranes, bones, and fluids to balance health and life force. I've studied manual therapies with the Upledger Institute since 2000 and with Chikly Institute since 2006.

Physiological blockages like inflammations and infections damage brain structure and function, affecting immunity, body structure, and the electromagnetic field.

Craniosacral and brain-lymph treatment yield excellent clinical results with inflammation, restriction, pain, and the adrenal exhaustion of FMS and CFS. They also add the elements of safety, nurturance, and touch, which help diffuse internal stress and the latent PTSD that began with ACEs. Craniosacral and brain-lymph therapies create significant transformation on numerous levels. Beyond the physical, when we touch the brain and membrane system, we are entering holy ground.

I love my patients. I see God in their faces and their form.

—A. T. Still, MD, DO

It may be a new concept for mainstream culture to imagine using manual assessment and treatment (bodywork!) for complex pain and disease, but people across all cultures have been doing this for as long as our species has been alive. Touch is a direct line of communication into the nervous system, with potent biochemical effects. The knowledge and practice of using touch to heal, held sacred by spiritual traditions throughout time, have been displaced by our modern medical ways. But the quantum sciences are evolving rapidly to reveal the interconnectedness of all things. Hands with refined perceptual sensitivity, like those of experienced bodyworkers, can perceive and neutralize disturbances at microscopic levels through the patient's electromagnetic energy field and help reorganize the patient's brain structure for resonance and healing. In section 3, we explored the physiology of light as the natural luminosity of our cellular matrix in its healthiest state. Science has detected yet another form of light in people, animals, and plants: *biophotons*. Physics discovered *biophoton emission*—the release of measurable frequencies of light from living things—about 150 years ago. We don't know the purpose of photon emission yet, but some scientists think it could signal nerve disturbance, much like the static I feel when I scan the client's body for clues.

According to GreenMed founder Sayer Ji, "Biophotons are emitted by the human body, can be released through mental intention, and may modulate fundamental processes within cell-to-cell communication and DNA." The research implies that biophoton exchanges occur between client and therapist to repair cellular damage. This factor alone should invite scientific inquiry because it implies that bodywork can affect mitochondrial health and metabolism and, in this way, serve to reverse chronic and degenerative disease.

When the nervous system is scrambled, nerve connectivity becomes scattered, disturbing our bioelectrical circuitry. This seems to be the case with sensitivity syndromes. Dysregulation of the electromagnetic field clouds our health and natural luminescence and makes it impossible to heal. Taking time in nature revives the nervous system and enhances our capacity to generate *and exchange* healing light. Spiritual practice does this as well. Light enlivens and heals. This is both literal and symbolic. Touch increases coherence, regeneration, and possibly even biophoton exchange, all of which awaken our innate power to heal.

All disease involves a blockage of flow on the physical level and an emotional disturbance holding it in place.

Early childhood trauma, especially when buried and forgotten, weakens the immune system, setting us up for illness later in life. Adverse childhood experiences, known in professional circles as ACEs, have been clinically studied, and the research is conclusive. ACEs are linked to a trajectory of demise throughout life, frequently marked by social withdrawal and latent PTSD. ACEs hypersensitize the nervous system to fear danger at all times. The physical and emotional scars of ACEs and other forms of trauma persist and can be triggered instantly by anything that the primal brain or that the immune system interprets as a potential threat.

Our bodies adapt magnificently for a long, long time, but eventually, the nervous system will become overwhelmed. It's impossible to hold pain, fear, and trauma inside us forever, and once we exceed the body's capacity to adapt, symptoms of disease appear—which is really the body's loud cry for help resetting itself. *Pharmaceutical intervention may or may not palliate, but it will never touch the issue's source.*

Our unconscious stores all its memories in the body tissues and the brain. Because we are primally and instinctually programmed to survive, negative memories and emotions form our dominant unconscious impressions, reactions, and beliefs. This could explain the underlying suspicion, tension, and agitation we see in the world all around us now. The unconscious stays busy reviewing its files and surfing the environment for potential danger. This creates enormous internal strain. At some point, the body, weakened and exhausted by excessive prolonged strain, reaches its breaking point. Old shadows burst through the surface of our awareness with volcanic force, insisting on being addressed. For resolution, somatic (body-based) healing practices like skilled bodywork, yoga, and massage are most effective. Psychiatrist Bessel Vanderkolk's research proved that these somatic connections are essential in healing trauma. Through bodywork and yoga, we learn to receive and then take conscious physical actions, gently enabling the body to discharge damaging emotions, reintegrate consciousness, and heal.

What is now known for sure is that neurological conditions compromise *all* systems of the body.

Neurologically, fibromyalgia and chronic fatigue are closely related, and their diagnoses are overlapping and complex. What is generally *not* understood, however, is that after all the medical tests are done and no virus, bacteria, or significant pathology is found, the **inflammation still remains in the cranial membranes and peripheral nerves,** and this alone will lead to a cascade of symptoms that all *seem* to have no cause.

Western medicine, with its symptomatic diagnosis and drugs, has no effective treatment for problems like these. For the patient to heal, we need to treat the brain inflammation first.

Ironically, pharmaceuticals tend to inflame the brain and nerves, further complicating the issue. Holistic doctors who work with the brain, gut, and autoimmune disorders are starting to point this out. In addition, there are psychological and emotional ramifications to suffering with FMS or CFS. Talk therapy alone will not help because the **body is holding the pain.** Hence, the body is where we need to start.

As a manual therapist, I've been blessed with gentle and effective assessment and treatment approaches that have no harsh side effects. I apply my hands, heart, soul intuition, intention, and three decades of training and experience in my work. Cranial, lymphatic, and osteopathic circles know that stagnation and inflammation resolve once physical structures are aligned to allow better drainage and flow; they also understand the power of skilled touch to spark healing. Self-healing becomes immediately possible once we mobilize the body's sacred fluids.

Revisiting Glia: The Brain Cells of Self-Repair

The brain's own self-repair system—**the glial cells**—is most active at night during REM sleep. This is why insomnia sufferers experience more inflammation and degeneration in addition to their pain and fatigue: they are not getting that time to heal. Inflammation and sleeplessness, common in neurological disorders, increase neurodegeneration measurably in the brain.

The glial brain cells are also known as the *glymphatic system* because they interface with the fluids in and around the brain and pass inflammatory waste products into the lymphatics to be cleared. Glia were first discovered in the 1800s but were until recently quite misunderstood. Glia were originally believed to be extracellular glue forming the matrix that interconnects regions of the brain. However, it is now known that they are integral to brain health, development, communication, and self-repair.

There are four main types of glial cells in the central (brain and spinal cord) and peripheral (body) nervous systems. While one type (oligodendrocytes) enhances brain communication by myelinating the brain and spinal cord, another (Schwann cells) myelinates the peripheral nerves. Myelin is the white sheath that covers nerve cells and nerve tracts, accelerating nerve conduction up to three hundred times. Astrocytes are the third glial cell type; they actively manage self-cleansing and self-repair. Lastly, microglia support the craniosacral system and cerebrospinal fluid flow.

The *glymphatic system* works most effectively at night. With deep sleep and healthy glial activation, painful symptoms recede like a wave, and brain degeneration can be influenced and even reversed.

For glial activation, once again, bodywork comes to the fore. Enhanced fluid flows and rapid intercommunication in and between the body and the brain make a world of difference in reversing pain and degeneration and increasing our overall ability to self-heal. But that's not all. Craniosacral and brain-lymph therapies, with their emphasis on focused intention and non-invasive subtle touch, help open glial pathways and optimize glial cell function. In fact, in advanced bodywork training, we learn to communicate clearly and compassionately with all parts of the body and the brain, and we teach our clients how to do the same.

Sensitivity Syndromes and Compassion

Neurological conditions are marked by confused nerve signaling and breakdowns in communication in the central nervous system, which consists of the spinal cord and brain. In this sense, all stress-related conditions are *neurological* in that they all involve the brain and nerves.

Fibromyalgia and chronic fatigue, which we've already covered, demonstrate progressive neural degeneration. We also touched on brain injuries earlier and explained how prolonged pain and buried trauma of any kind weaken the structures and functions of the brain. In each of these examples, nerve conduction is interrupted as synapses shrivel and myelin sheaths start to thin and fray. When the nerve cells are injured, they become feeble and raw, so a certain amount of hypersensitivity is common in any relentless condition.

At the physiological level, all of life is *neurological.*

Our physical and emotional experiences, which include our escalating pain levels, reactions, and beliefs about healing, are reflected in and expressed through the brain and spinal nerves. As mentioned, chronic illness leads to—and may evolve from—early trauma and emotional distress. We tend to feel shame, anxiety, and depression and to self-isolate as a result. Isolation itself disconnects and damages the brain. This trajectory of emotional suffering and withdrawal happen with sensitivity syndromes too. Understanding the challenges and struggles these conditions entail can help us feel more compassion for ourselves and others when we get stuck feeling unwell and just can't seem to initiate change. Each of us is doing the best we can to learn, grow, and keep up with the times. It's worth mentioning that there are health benefits to letting go of judgment and blame.

When Gregg Braden met with high lamas in remote monasteries in Tibet, he asked what holds the universe together, and they told him this: compassion. Buddhist monks spend their lives meditating on compassion. Compassion, more than a feeling, is a coherent and transformative energy field that unifies and heals.

Brain research now links compassion with highly integrated brain function, strong immune resistance, and lasting states of joy. *Self-compassion, and compassion for others, accelerates healing!*

If you are reading this book, you yourself may be sensitive or empathic and feel life *too* deeply—a blessing that in this world often masquerades as a curse. It's easy to blame and punish ourselves when we don't measure up in the harshness of the world.

May what follows reveal a new perspective on sensitivity, empathy, and suffering and clearly demonstrate that an open and sensitive nervous system is the direct line to spirit and the voice of the soul.

Sensitivity is a blessing because it makes the veil very thin. Intuition and subtle perception are easy and naturally enhanced.

Still, **Highly Sensitive People** (HSPs) suffer immensely in a world that can feel harsh, loud, and crude. They have fewer emotional filters and are acutely aware of everything around them, including the thoughts and emotions of everyone else. **Empaths** are highly sensitive. So are **mystics.** *Hypersensitivity also results from buried trauma and the residual brain distortion and shrinkage that occur.* Myelin loss is evident in neurodegenerative diseases like Alzheimer's, Parkinson's, and Autism, which means the nerves in the brain become increasingly stripped and raw. Hypersensitivity results there as well. Yet another sensitivity syndrome that involves hypersensitivity and extreme fragility in the nervous system is **Hypermobility Disorder**. (HMD) is a lesser-known condition with its own distinct set of traits, which will be discussed separately later on.

Meditative awareness, self-compassion, and lifestyle skills are important energetic shields to prevent hypersensitivity from progressing into an illness or from seeming to blast us apart. This really pertains to all of us, but it applies most urgently to those plagued by sensitivity syndromes.

Sensitivity disorders have appeared increasingly over the last few decades, yet still remain relatively unknown. Because they are invisible in third-dimension reality (the realm of matter), those who suffer from sensitivities have been misdiagnosed, medicated, and deemed mentally ill. As long as Western medicine rejects the energetic causes of pain and disease—which are highlighted throughout this book— patients will suffer needlessly, and neurodegenerative illnesses will continue to progress.

There is an upsurge in sensitivity on the planet now, for better and for worse. If we can consider the possibility that sensitivity is the spiritual gift it can actually be, then we can unleash its raw power to help us all heal.

Chronic hyperstimulation overwhelms our neural circuits, creating heat and inflammation in the brain.

In harsh, abrasive environments like cities, our nerves really can and do become frayed. With rising epidemics of environmental illness, the big picture seems hopeless, but it also makes a lot more sense. There is a limit to the amount of input and stimulation the human nervous system can take before needing to quietly assimilate. Being overwhelmed makes the brain shut down; we are fundamentally wired to survive. Self-preservation is a pure and natural biological response. Although we appear to adapt, we eventually lose our tolerance and capacity to bear the noise, traffic, pollution, radiation, chemicals, and stressful overstimulation of modern life.

The nervous system struggles heroically to adapt, so most of us remain unaware of blaring media messages, noise pollution, and bad smells. Still, these invasive energies disturb and disable brain and nerve transmission and slow the body's ability to respond—physically and cognitively. This creates a deep, rumbling stress and panic inside, which may be unconscious, but nonetheless, it breaks us down, setting the stage for brain and nerve degeneration.

Wired for survival, we unconsciously learn to guard and block, and some of our methods are not the best for our health. However, compassion, meditation, spiritual practice, and self-care are like protective shields, enabling us to find deep resilience instead. For many of us, meditation provides a respite because it neutralizes emotions, cools the brain, and creates a sense of spaciousness within. As we see in highly trained yogis, shamans, and monks, committed spiritual practice strengthens and refines the brain and nerves. When we meditate, we find sanctuary for a while and emerge feeling less assaulted by the cacophonous roar and pressure of the world.

Everything in life has cumulative effects over time: pain and sadness, faith and optimism, education and health. Meditation and bodywork strengthen our adaptability and resilience, establishing strong brain connectivity and accelerating neuroplasticity in evolutionary ways. Mystics of all spiritual traditions understood and benefitted from this dynamic, and now scientific research on brain healing finally concurs. We can reshape and strengthen our brains, and broken nerves can regenerate and heal.

Hypersensitivity: Highly Sensitive People and Empaths

Many among us simply don't have thick enough skin for the noise and pressure of the world. The sensitive and empathic among us long to drift into a more soulful and imaginal world, where gentleness and creativity are valued and expressed. Compassion is natural for HSPs—highly sensitive people. We are pulled by our hearts and willing to cross all human boundaries to help others, too often draining ourselves. Then we have to retreat because we have emptied ourselves by giving too much. The soul of humanity is bursting across the planet now to answer the call of the times. Hypersensitivity and extreme empathy are a normal part of life for many people today. Yet, these traits can take their toll. People with special sensitivities can do all the right things and still not feel well - until they learn to give themselves the quiet time they really need to soothe and replenish their brains.

This is our *choice point* in history, as Gregg Braden often points out in these very words. The future is up to each of us.

In the Chinese language, *crisis* means much more than *opportunity;* it designates a choice point—the eye of the needle we must pass through for our survival and the better times to come. This world sorely needs gentle, sensitive souls to balance the tides of degradation and destruction all around us now. It's time to honor our sensitivity as a gift of grace and to nurture it as the blessing it can become.

It's no accident that there are now expanding numbers of hypersensitive souls. As we've seen, numerous circumstances can create highly attuned neural sensitivity. Prolonged stress, trauma, pain, neurodegeneration, hypermobility, hyperempathy, ACEs, and birth karma are a few.

People in these categories develop keen awareness above and beyond the accepted norms and often suffer as a result. At the physical level, sensitivity syndromes can all manifest as pain, agitation, or disease.

Highly sensitive people and empaths are like finely tuned radio antennas that pick up all stations at once.

This is overwhelming, and they quickly lose themselves in the roar and the din. With constant stimulation bombarding their attention, they never truly get to rest. They remain amped up and hypervigilant, brains hot and nerves raw. For this reason, HSPs and empaths tend to be chronically anxious, overspent, and run-down. These people also commonly develop allergies, sleep and digestive disorders, emotional instability, and chronic pain. In addition, they are frequently invalidated, and even mocked, for feeling and smelling things that nobody else can. Public places are challenging, and the energy of large crowds is painful to their nerves.

Many people with sensitivity syndromes are introverts in what feels like a very noisy world, and their talents are rarely acknowledged or respected. Being diminished in this way increases depression and social withdrawal. Highly sensitive people and empaths express their brilliance and creativity more quietly. To be truly healthy and happy, those with sensitive nervous systems need regular down time to rebalance and reset.

I notice in clinical practice that symptoms like chronic pain and anxiety always correlate with a highly sensitized nervous system and a speedy, overheated brain. The bottom line is to quiet the brain and learn what calm actually feels like. But it's also really important to support and encourage the sensitivity. Sensitivity enables the soul to perceive truth as the voice of inner guidance speaks.

Hypermobility Syndromes: Bodies Without Brakes

In recent years, neurology has validated a puzzling connective tissue disease that disrupts the central nervous system and impacts neuromuscular control: Ehlers-Danlos syndromes (EDS).

EDS is a massive category, and this genetic collagen disorder is the least understood type. The hypermobility (excessive flexibility) spectrum of EDS has multiple names: **hypermobility syndrome** (HMS), **hypermobility disorder** (HMD), and **joint hypermobility syndrome** (JHS). I was recently informed that the name has been simplified to **hypermobile EDS,** or hEDS, but all names still apply and are used interchangeably, depending on the source. New research findings come out every day.

I prefer the term *HMS*. Language influences our consciousness and perception in subtle ways, which either supports our health or adversely affects our ability to heal. In my estimation, the word *syndrome* opens up hope; it sounds transient and approachable, while *disorder* does not. On the **HMS** spectrum, *the whole fascial web* is too flexible—it's not only the ligaments and joints. For this reason as well, ***hypermobility syndrome*** is a more accurate term. It's a condition where everything in the body stretches too much, and sufferers struggle constantly to keep their bones and joints in place. Aside from the variety of genetic collagen aberrations found, ED is a mystery, and neurologists say there is no cure. People on the hED spectrum lack the structural support that healthy fascia—connective tissue—provides. They have no end range when they stretch, and they often get injured by going too far.

Flexibility can be pathological. *Yes, it's true.*

Hypermobile people have defective collagen and loose ligaments. The body's collagen matrix is dysfunctionally weak, so it can't support structure and movement, and joints easily slip out of place. Meanwhile, the muscles and nerves are constantly strained by trying to stabilize their loose parts. HMS/ED is an autonomic nervous system disturbance; the body becomes too stressed to self-regulate and maintains a high sympathetic nervous system tone—a constant internal state of fight or flight. This emergency response opposes parasympathetic relaxation and therefore blocks healing.

HMS/EDS brings other surprising nervous system complications, such as **headaches, palpitations, anxiety, cold hands and feet, digestive disorders, dizziness, lightheadedness, organ prolapse, confusion, and dyslexia with numbers and sequences.** Strain, dislocation, exhaustion, and collapse are real and ever-present threats with pathological HMS. Compensatory muscles spasm throughout the body to stabilize the joints, fueling endless cycles of strain, pain, anxiety, panic, and low-grade PTSD.

This is vital to understand. *HMS is a nervous system imbalance,* so medicating these individual symptoms does not touch the cause, and patients will continue to get worse—while jeopardizing their livers with the pharmaceutical drugs. What is needed is a holistic approach to treating the nervous system as a whole. Presenting that has been the goal of this book.

Although many hypermobile people do live perfectly functional lives, many more do not. HMS sufferers have poor *proprioception*—the inner sense of where their bodies are in space. Their nervous systems are delicate, and any kind of stress or strain can potentially be too much. This includes *normal* activities like exercise, long work days, moving furniture around, and lifting and carrying babies, boxes, and bags. According to EDS specialist and craniosacral therapist Eloise Stager, roughly 2 percent of HMS sufferers are at the extreme end of the spectrum: they are so structurally unstable that their joints dislocate doing common everyday things, like stepping off a curb or picking up a cup. HMS people all struggle with unbearable, unexplainable symptoms every day and tend to "hurt for no reason" much or all of the time. It is estimated that about 20 percent of the population fits somewhere on the HMS spectrum, and others may remain misdiagnosed or undiagnosed. Only in recent years did neurologists acknowledge hypermobility as a real pathology. It went unrecognized for centuries because it is invisible, and its symptoms overlap with those found in the aforementioned central sensitivity syndromes, trauma, and chronic pain. In the past, HMS patients were diagnosed with hysteria or mental illness—which also happened for centuries with fibromyalgia and chronic fatigue.

In most cases, hypermobility causes constant injury, strain, pain, and loss of function, with cumulative effects over time.

It also seems that hED can precipitate or accompany fibromyalgia or chronic fatigue. Hypermobile patients have to learn how to hold back, or they suffer.. Because of poor proprioception (the sense of our body's orientation in space), they can't tell how far they've stretched and don't feel the strain until later on.

Proprioception can be learned with patient coaching that reinforces the safe end range of movement. Once HMS people learn to limit moving into dislocation, strain, and pain, they can avoid injuring themselves. Helping these clients learn about and stabilize their bodies is a joy for me. I see when someone has excessive flexibility right away, and it's immensely gratifying to help people get out of pain.

The struggle to hold joints in place can be a full-time job that takes energy and zaps strength. Hypermobile bodies *have no brakes*.

Because the body of a sufferer lacks normal structural restrictions and fascial support, hypermobility is not the blessing onlookers imagine it to be. HMS demands rigorous awareness to avoid chronic injury and destabilization and to keep up with life. There is a learning curve to proprioception and movement, and there are wisdom and encouragement to be gained along the way.

Hypermobile people do not need to stretch. They need to stabilize.

Yoga needs a new language for students with HMS. Hearing the word *stretch* in every yoga class they attend, and being praised for their flexibility, leads HMS sufferers further into injury, chronic pain, anxiety, self-anger, and self-blame. Most yoga teachers have no idea this condition exists. *I hope they all find this book!*

In my thirty years of teaching yoga, about half my students and clients had some degree of previously unrecognized hypermobility. All except for one were women, and they were basically functional, except for the frequent episodes of pain that their unstable bodies caused. More women than men are hypermobile. It could be hormonal, or maybe because women focus more on flexibility than men, they naturally "embody" it more.

Hypermobility usually develops early in life. Our body structure is shaped largely by how we use it. Women are encouraged to pursue flexibility. In youth and adolescence, the brain and body are still forming. If we knew what to look for, we would probably notice hypermobile tendencies around this time. Baseline body tone is established in our formative years, prior to puberty and into adolescence, when hormones surge. If more attention goes to range of motion than to alignment, young women with hypermobile tendencies may innocently stretch too far and get hurt.

HMS people can regulate strain and pain by not exceeding the limits of their strength.

Tissue that stretches too much is not strong; in its excess flexibility, it's lax. To avoid pain, HMS people need to contain their movements (hold back) and slowly build their strength. In the beginning, it can be frustrating because there's no sensory awareness of exactly where that arm or leg is or how to organize the spinal curves. But core alignment can be learned, and it's well worth the time and focus that it demands.

In the long run, HMS presents the same deep nerve exhaustion as CFS. For instance, when hypermobile people work out in the gym, or when they lift, drag, or carry heavy things, it exhausts their chronically strained bodies, and they may relapse afterward into pain and fatigue for days or weeks at a time. This is not their fault; they've exceeded what their body structure can support. The best gift to a hypermobile person is someone—a teacher or therapist—who sees the problem and helps define the terrain.

Too many hypermobile people end up bedridden for long periods of their lives, unable to work or get through a normal day. Some end up in wheelchairs because the pain gets so bad. Although a classified neurological disorder of the connective tissue, HMS is still relatively unknown. The medical community at large is completely unaware.

Here's one subject's story:

> At age twenty, I became disabled and spent two years in bed. After many long years of recovery, I relapsed again in 2016.
>
> I started trying to reverse my own hypermobility when I was twenty-two, but I had no idea back then what it was. I had terrible headaches, severe body pain that moved around and incapacitated me, and I felt sick and hung over almost all the time. My hips, back, and legs burned, and it was hard to stand up at all. There were long periods of time when my sacrum would slip sideways, and my pelvis got

locked at some strange angle that left me unable to move at all. Everything I did with my body cost me days in bed, and sometimes it can still be that way. But not all the time now like it was then.

Back then, my whole nervous system would freeze, my back would lock, and I had to wait it out. Then, anytime I could move, I used adrenaline to get me around before my body crashed again. This went on for thirty years.

My arms and legs bend—in all directions—far too much. My yoga teachers saw it all but couldn't help me, so they encouraged me to work to heal it myself. It was frustrating and devastating all the time to have no real support—from my body, or from any other human—and to have to tackle this alone. When just getting through the day at all is an astronomical feat, it's hard to find energy for anything else, but I kept my sights on the highest star and wrestled optimism back to life every day. Many days, I failed at this, but I knew I could not give up. If nobody else could help me, that must mean that I could fix it myself!

Starting in the dark before dawn, I would focus my consciousness to therapeutically influence my agonized body every day—for over thirty years! Then in 2016, out of the blue, it hit hard in a new way. I looked up one day, and a sharp jolt blasted my pelvis straight through the hip joints; then my hips gave out. Suddenly, I couldn't stand or walk at all. When I looked within, I sensed that the joints were grinding bone on bone and slicing into nerves. Every moment was so agonizing that my ability to focus was completely subsumed. If I rested a lot, I could work a little, and to do this, I had to sit and lean to balance my weight away from the worst of the pain. This went on for two solid years while I willed myself all day, every day, to see it healed so I could have a life again. The mental battles were violent and loud for twenty-four months. My emotions crashed frequently as I fought off the images of wheelchairs and permanent disability and instead meditated to build new cartilage and bone. My first goals were humble: to park my car, to walk down the block, and to work even half a day. The high bar was to leave this suffering far behind me, build my healing business, and hike and dance again. I got acupuncture a lot, showed up in my meditation chair every day before dawn, and found ways to serve my church. In the midst of such overwhelming torment, I did not feel like a blessed child of the divine, and I blamed myself. I knew this was wrong thinking, so I began to explore unusual types of therapy to help turn my attitude and emotions around. I reminded myself to receive the love from my friends. Then finally, in October 2018, I met the low bar and began to walk the treadmill and hike a little. It's still a constant battle of ups and downs, and I often get too tired and overwhelmed before my day is done, but as long as I can get up again, I win. Now in my meditations, I'm more positive, and praise my hips for their achievement and my body for its wondrous ability to self-heal. Now I'm calling forth new stem cells from my brain and bones to feed my hips - and I revel in gratitude, no matter what.

This story is an ongoing saga that has challenged, educated, and formed me over the years; and I confess, it is my own.

My clinical expertise in hypermobility is professional and intimately personal as well. I'm dangerously hypermobile myself. I've lived with the extremes of pain and disability from HMS since I was twenty years old; in other words, for my entire adult life. There are a lot of bad days, but it used to be weeks and months of inflammation before I could move again. The disabling episodes resolve faster now. I'm wiser and more experienced today. Much more patient too!

> Those who survive the journey to the underworld earn the right to teach.

> —Caroline Casey

Yoga is evolutionary. Awareness transforms.

I was steeped in yoga practice long before my injury, so it never occurred to me that I would give it up. I haven't.

When yoga dawned on me as a small child, I understood it as a call to mastery and said yes. I intuited that yoga had called me to a path of power; that body mastery was involved; and that every day I would need to pay attention and take another step. As of this writing, I've practiced daily for almost fifty years, and my practices are as varied and diverse as yoga itself. Yoga was teaching me long before I ever had a teacher, or this practice even had a name. Yoga was and is my life partner, the most insistent longing in my heart.

Since my twenties, thanks to yoga, I have used conscious focus to hold my bones together in every moment, and to put my full awareness behind every movement I make. *Healing is a practice of mindfulness.* Now I use all that I've learned to help others heal their bodies and become whole.

As a child, I wanted to inspire people when I grew up. Yoga dawned spontaneously within me as a clear vision of possibility for humankind. I was prompted through inner guidance alone to practice asana, and I trusted that understanding would come in time. I had no idea back then that flexibility could be a problem, because flexibility is generally considered impressive and desirable in our world. In my own family, this was certainly the case.

In retrospect, I can track my hypermobility back to my teens; and now I see the role it played in my four decades of disability and pain. When I was twenty-four, my first yoga teacher advised me to "put the brakes on" and tasked me to figure out the *how* for myself. I was angry at my situation, yet determined. Since then, my yoga asana practice has focused on alignment, joint stabilization, and core strength, and I use props for support. I stopped going to classes twenty years ago because I was crippled after every class. The general approach in public classes doesn't work for hyper mobile bodies. Long deep stretches, deep lunges, and holding standing poses a long time disables us. After public classes I couldn't walk for two weeks, and that seemed an extreme price to pay. So since then I've mostly practiced on my own.

Hypermobility is an invisible condition wrought by unimaginable pain. The way modern yoga classes emphasize flexibility and strength can be destructive for HMS. Well-meaning yoga teachers push our bodies and nervous systems into overwhelm with deep stretches, deep lunges, and long holding times. I love yoga dearly and have never been willing or able to give it up. I use chairs and blankets because my body does not permit me to hold deep poses for long periods without support. If I do, I'll come apart later in the day, and endure strain and dislocation for days or weeks. In all my years of intensively focused microalignment to set my body straight, I never imagined HMS could lead to joint degeneration and nerve damage, *but now I understand that it can.* The collagen in our ligaments, tendons, and fascia provides structural support, cushioning, and bounce. In normal bodies, it springs back after being stretched. HMS lacks the needed collagen structure, so the support and resilience normally provided by fascia, tendons, and ligaments is not available to us.

Even in my fifties, I am still learning from day to day how to hold back and remembering to ask my body what it needs and how much it can do. Three essential life support tools for hypermobility are attitude, inner awareness, and alignment, so I emphasize these things. Then I ask myself what's possible; I try not to look at all the things that hurt too much. Can I call forth stem cells and make new collagen? Can I replace the cartilage in my synovial joints and regenerate the nerves? Can I recover my athletic ability at this age? Epigenetics suggests the answer to all these questions is yes, and to discover this is my personal and professional quest. It's always a test of patience, but maybe compassion and wisdom are finally dawning now.

I notice we tend to get angry at our bodies when they don't perform as we expect. Seeing this anger rise in my clients who struggle with pain helps me see it in myself as well. Anger strains our hearts and poisons our blood. Anger also neuroplasticizes the brain to favor negativity, pain, and disease. I used to criticize and blame myself harshly when my body would crash and burn all the time, and now I realize this attitude only accelerates degeneration and prolongs pain. Though we may have never thought of it this way before, this is an important lesson for us all on the value of compassion in brain development and in healing.

What sensitivity syndromes ask of us is compassion. Compassion is a powerfully influential force in the world. By projecting compassion outward, we contribute to peace and healing in the world. But to carry this blessing, we must first be willing to care kindly for ourselves. We begin to heal and bless others when we turn compassion toward ourselves.

At first glance, sensitivity syndromes may seem unrelated. Yet, when we pay attention, we see how nervous system imbalance, emotions, and beliefs keep us stuck. We also start to notice the tension and compression in our body posture that is holding our painful memories, emotions, and beliefs in place. Although this could apply to any of us, unconscious holding patterns seem especially prevalent in sensitivity syndromes like chronic fatigue, fibromyalgia, hypermobility, PTSD, and degenerative neurological disorders. Resolution comes by addressing physical structure, emotions, residual trauma, and beliefs.

Bodies don't come with instructions. Pain and illness bring up deep fear because we don't understand how our bodies work. Fear blocks life force, and healing energy *is* life force, so fear disrupts healing.

The better we understand how our bodies work, the faster we can access life force. This begins with awareness and a simple willingness to feel the discomfort, fear, and self-doubt. Holistic medicine and energy medicine are grounded in nature. Reconnection with the flow of our own life force transforms our entire relationship with life. Through the therapeutic process, we discover how much power we really do have—and we learn to express it.

My quantum approach to wellness contains three main branches: bodywork, yoga, and plant medicine. These lifestyle practices guide us gently from within, building our awareness, self-knowledge, and life force. Bodywork radically accelerates the healing process, reconnecting us with our body structure and our inner circuitry with the cosmic grid. Yoga asana practice provides anatomy knowledge *experientially* and develops our focus and intention. Knowledge empowers our confidence and ability, while focus and intention determine outcomes. The third branch of holistic healing I endorse is herbalism. I only use natural medicine; the pharmaceuticals I was given as a child made me sick and gave me bruises, so I've always researched plants and herbs. I don't go to Western doctors or take prescription drugs. Since becoming a certified herbalist in 2012, I make herbal oils, salves, and tinctures for myself, my clients and my friends. I rely completely on plants and herbs every day for medicine, nutrition, and emergency first aid, and I specialize in herbal preparations for soft tissue, bone, and joint repair.

To self-heal is to self-transform and live life in a more mindful, meditative way.

Meditative awareness brings hope and healing. We hear the voice of guidance whispering within—which the roar of public opinion will always oppose. Yet eventually, pain slows us down and points us toward inner reflection—the first bridge to self-transformation and true health. Meditation and yoga keep us reflectively engaged and awake. Meditation is a time to listen to the quiet voice within. Meditative awareness also supports us to act on our bodies' wisdom. Following the inner guidance we receive, even when the mind questions, balks, and doubts, is the second bridge to transformation and health. The third bridge is to attend to the body itself and to hear the story our postural alignment tells. In the manual therapy field, we say, "The issues are in the tissues," and somatic psychology research and our newest treatment protocols all agree.

Alignment therapies can prevent and reverse degenerative conditions, and this has been the focus of my career. Therapeutic alignment diminishes stresses on the bones and joints and increases the systemic circulation of fluids. NeuroMuscular Therapy (NMT) is a deep tissue style of medical massage that realigns the body region by region, integrating posture and movement to eliminate pain. More gentle and subtle, Craniosacral Therapy (CST) and brain-lymph work address membrane compression and cranial bone alignment, increasing oxygen, fluid flows, and brain integration. Subtle work eliminates internal pressure and strain, often enabling body structure to self-correct without the use of deep tissue massage.

Postural distortions stress our joints, which both causes and exacerbates bone and joint disorders.

Let's look briefly at a few extremely common pathologies as examples. **Bunions** of the feet, **stenosis** (of the neck or low back), and **arthritis** are types of abnormal bone growth. Here's what they share: they are all adaptations to chronic strain, overuse, and subtle misalignments. Perhaps long ago, there was an injury that never quite healed, or pain that altered the position of the bones. The body lays down extra calcium where it experiences strain, and that calcium accumulates over time and hardens as new bone. Just as they appear with strain, calcium deposits can disappear as body alignment shifts. Extra calcium can be dissolved and reabsorbed by the body when it is no longer needed for support.

Realignment therapies center both the mind and the body, which clarifies our focus and increases life force right away. Human anatomy is an intricate and perfectly interconnected machine. Alignment places the brain and nerves in proper physical relationship for balance and communication to take place. Realignment is soul work, because our sense of center is not just physical or random. We create new alignment with consistent, gentle meditative focus, and in doing so, we find new resonance in ourselves. In a state of harmony, we enter quantum reality, where self-healing and evolution naturally occur.

****

Yoga's Deeper Inquiry: Do You Believe You Can Heal?

The real question at hand here is, *"Do you believe you can heal?"*

Our culture has been inculcated with disempowering beliefs. How many people always call the doctor first? That's conditioning, like Pavlov's dogs. How many times do we hear of a medical prognosis delivered with discouragement and lack of hope, and the person just gives up? That's conditioning too. Our brains are set between birth and age seven, during which time we are completely permeable to incoming thoughts and beliefs. Throughout life, our brains will use this information to scan for danger. New beliefs are formed that will keep us safe. The power of unconscious beliefs to rule our lives is not just talk any more. In order to heal ourselves, we must first know with certainty that we can; and then discard any thoughts and beliefs that conflict with this truth. It's time to examine how we act out our unconscious conditioning, and where fear blocks our conviction that we can heal. We have to look within.

Yoga is an introspective evolutionary science.

Yoga, in its true sense, means living life with intentional connection - to our bodies, thoughts, lifestyles, and emotions - as well as to whatever we consider to be the divine God force and our source of spiritual support. This connection provides extraordinary power and resilience in life. Yoga has little to do with *stretching*. Flexibility is a wonderful and important benefit of yoga practice, but not its essence. Connection is the essence.

We may miss yoga's connection to spirit by focusing on externals. Yoga is a practice of awareness, rich with life force and untapped potential. Yoga is a lifelong relationship with ourselves and what might be possible beyond the limited human mind.

I taught public yoga classes in yoga studios for thirty years. It seemed that most people came once or once in a while and had little interest in the self-healing process that Yoga is. Perhaps by now that has changed. It was hard to deliver an entire body of knowledge with erratic waves of attendance. It felt incomplete, and keeping up with this eventually wore me out. In any healing process, relationship and consistency matter; trust and teamwork can move enormous mountains aside. In large groups, we are not seen; and doing everything by ourselves online, we miss the depth and intimacy of transformation. I have one ongoing yoga group now, and we've been working together for ten years. They are dedicated, persistent, and inspiring active women around the age of seventy. When they sprain an ankle, tear a shoulder, or have surgery, they heal fast. *How?* They know and believe they can heal, and stay loyal to their relationship with yoga and themselves. They attend our sessions and other public classes, and also show up almost every day on their mats at home.

"Do you believe you can heal?"

Many of us never stop to consider the messages and beliefs our bodies hold. The question of *whether we really believe we are capable of healing* is fundamental to the outcome of any efforts we make. If this question meets a blank stare, we're not even in the same stadium to play this game. Without determination and absolute faith in the life force within, there's nothing anyone can add. Healing is not something that is "done *to* us"; we have to choose to be *all-in*. The power already there inside us is ready to dramatically change our lives. Holistic medicine and spiritual practices help set it free.

Yoga is a perfect testing ground for how much faith we have in our ability to heal. It brings challenges for the human body and mind. As someone who has lived with pain and disability for almost forty years, I've been tested on most days of my life. This has cultivated my patience and insight into the pain and disability that others face, along with my ability to channel healing force. Ultimately, I know that potentially each and every one of us can heal. It's only a question of who will step onto the path. The practice chose me; I was "drafted" as a child.

My yoga story started when I was young, with visions and sensations that compelled my asana practice for fourteen years. I finally met my yoga teachers in 1983–84, and we stayed connected for many years—long past my first Iyengar Yoga teaching certificate in 1992. My teachers had clear perception and subtle awareness. They knew how to read bodies and accurately assess from observation where someone would feel pain and what new movement patterns could bring change. Their accuracy was stunning and immensely desirable to me. They spotted my hyper mobility early on, and when none of the techniques or experts they introduced me to could help, or even made me worse, they asked me to cure it myself. That felt like my only choice. In spite of the grueling pain throughout all this time and beyond, I never gave up, because I sincerely believed my body could heal itself. In the long run, Iyengar Yoga did not suit my body, and after 25 years I chose to let it go. Iyengar Yoga gave me a powerful introduction to the anatomy of yoga that is forever emblazoned on my being, along with imprints of my teachers, whom I dearly love.

When we land on a path, we may devote years to that relationship, only to find that it's a temporary passage or not right *for us at all;* but in the midst of the struggle, we open new pathways and learn about ourselves. During more than thirty years of frequent and disabling pain, Mr. Iyengar's pictures in *Light on Yoga* were my vision of possibility. Two quotes from the book have lived with me all along as mandates for my life. They succinctly express the assignment before us all now on the yogic path.

> The body is my temple, and asanas are my prayers.
>
> —BKS Iyengar

> The purpose of Yoga is to bring light to every cell.
>
> —BKS Iyengar

Through his words and masterful images, Mr. Iyengar radiates the power of yoga to embody light.

Asanas are vectors of light projecting into the cosmic grid, luminous threads of connection and integration with the cosmic web.

Beyond all the intensive training, detailed instructions, sequencing, and form, I honor yoga for the possibility to radiate light. As discussed earlier, the vibrational frequency of light transmits potent healing force. Mr. Iyengar so simply and humbly exemplified this.

Seeking to live by these two quotes myself, I've experienced prayer *beyond the body* within my asana practice and have touched that light our yoga practice can transmit. Through my body, injured as it has been, I've felt energy follow the shapes of the poses, and divine light growing within. In those moments of grace, flow and connection, there is no pain. Devotion to yoga is the gift of power and peace.

We are antennas. The human nervous system is the main receiver and conductor of universal electromagnetic force.

Yoga postures are sacred geometries that weave us into the grid of reality, the quantum field. The energy body in yoga - the *chakra system* - is sourced within *sushumna,* the central channel. *Sushumna* correlates to our craniosacral system: the brain, spinal cord, and its fluid-filled membranes. Through the electroconductivity of the nervous system, each of us is threaded as light crystals into the divine whole. In the poetry of the mystics, we are each stars and galaxies in the quantum field. Exploring interconnectedness through yoga awakens inner light. Gently aligning the spine in every pose allows us to carry and embody this light in physical form. There is no one perfect way to do any pose or one single precise version of any position that everyone should pursue. The nuances of alignment are unique to each of us. Like our fingerprints, our body structure, posture, and movement patterns are one of a kind. We overcome self-judgment and the illusion of perfection when we approach yoga in this way.

Alignment is never purely physical. It reverberates infinitely.

Alignment is prayer. It opens our inner channels to the divine. In Yoga, we gratefully and prayerfully encourage those instants of connection and flow that bring us closer to ourselves. Alignment restores our clarity, sense of center, and physical stability. Tiny shifts in physical position (micro-movements) affect whole body alignment *and consciousness* right away. The nervous system is synchronized when strain and pressure are relieved. The electromagnetic field (aura) expands. Alignment is an evolutionary skill. Structure matters.

Asana—practicing postures—was the main branch of my Yoga practice for many years. It was always in my consciousness as a longing and a memory that first appeared as visions and sensations when I was a child. Though I didn't know there was a thing called *yoga* when I was young, its power penetrated me and endures to this day. My relationship with yoga and the postures was completely experiential and self-revealing. Yoga taught me to meditate and exposed me to all that it is. Asana connects neural circuits and sensory experience, and I feel I've touched eternities in mystic space. During all those years of injuries and disability, I would superimpose imprints of impeccable poses over my fractured self in meditation, with absolute faith that I would eventually heal. Life tests our limits, and the body regenerates itself continually with our attention and support. Yoga tests the limits of our consciousness to reorganize matter, and the gift of neuroplasticity enables us to succeed.

Everything is alive and interconnected. Even quantum particles interact and co-create across time and space. It's time in history to lean into this connection and use it to co-create. But first, we must clear ourselves to open the way. By releasing pain and static from the sacred body vessel, we enter a state of *yoga*—sacred union—with all life.

The practice of Yoga has to become our own. Teachers provide outward reflection, inspiration, and support, but they can't replace the power of listening to the body and learning to act from within.

So again I ask, do you believe you can heal? If so, then let's begin.

Grounding, Centering, and Yoga

To speak of grounding and centering invokes images of great old trees solidly rooted into the earth. As ancient and primal vessels and channels between heaven and earth, trees are reminders of the possibility for all of life to attain uninterrupted relationship with the One.

For living beings, Earth is the source of life. Our very breath comes out of her, as do food, shelter, and tools.

Whether or not we realize it, we are born of the same raw material as stars in the galaxy. We share the same reality of constant evolution and change. Earth sustains our lives and reminds us that wholeness and connection are real. When we disconnect from nature, we become sick and depressed. To seek connection with our very blood, bones and breath brings yoga alive.

Yoga is wholeness in a fragmented world. It's not an exercise; it's a state of being.

These are delicate and fragile times. All of life feels the weight of the *now*. Embodiment gives us a chance to ground and center here on earth, along with the challenge to connect and transcend. To pursue our true potential honors our birthright and strengthens the tapestry of our world.

There is greatness within each of us, which has coalesced uniquely over many lifetimes by design or divine chance. Yoga practice cultivates consciousness to nurture and reveal our unique gifts. Postures are a small piece of the science of yoga, yet by attending to the physical body we serve the full embodiment of the soul.

Whether we recognize the field of magnetic energy sustaining us or merely feel the challenge of lifting against gravity into handstand, we are right. We may assume that yoga only stretches our arms, legs, or toes, but when we are grounded in the body and freely breathing, we slip naturally into *heart-brain coherence—inner harmony*. Then, we can access and awaken the transformative energies latent within us. When we are connected, the forces of creation surge through us and quantum evolution naturally occurs.

Spiritual Surges and Conscious Evolution Today

There is an unseen tidal wave pouring across the globe right now, and it's not what most people would think. This energy is volcanic. It has no visible form to the common eye. There are no words to describe it yet, and it erupts from deep inside each one of us.

Spiritual Force

Spiritual force is the energy of creation—what some call Source or Higher Power and others know as God—and in whom some adepts see Kundalini Mata Shakti dancing the 108 gestures of transformation on the planet with Shiva all the time. Spiritual force is the living God/dess on holy fire, along with the sudden earth changes that are doing wild cartwheels on our heads. Spiritual force is how evolution takes form.

Meanwhile, in our daily lives, we are grieving astronomical losses while carrying on our insanely busy, stressful lives. Grief and stress leave gaping holes if they are not made whole again. The traditions of Yoga have an infinite array of paths to bliss. Chanting, breathing, praying, dancing, reading sacred scripture, and practicing asana are just a few. Our souls long for the ultimate possible human experience of union and oneness. It changes us for the better.

Explosive bliss is programmed genetically into our brains. Bliss is an essential nutrient for health and survival.

We humans have natural **endocannabinoid systems in our brains and our guts** that produce and transmit **hormones of bliss.** We make these hormones ourselves and have the perfectly shaped receptors for them too.

Bliss lifts us. Bliss expands us into possibility. Bliss helps us heal.

As Gregg Braden explains in *Secrets of the Lost Mode of Prayer,* when we combine thoughts, feelings, intentions, and beliefs, we breathe life into our prayer. Bringing the prayer to life enhances our biological alignment with infinity, possibility, and expansion. In the prayerful presence of spirit, the immune system and emotions thrive. Connection is a vitalizing and healing balm. Connected through the spiritual force of our prayer, we become filled and overflowing with love. Our presence blesses, and moment by moment, we create the world we want to live in and see.

Yoga is a consciousness exercise that connects us to spiritual force. Just by turning our attention inward, we can transform thoughts, doubts, and fears into spiritual force to energize and heal. The same energy that reformulates a limiting belief can rebuild a broken bone. Yet, in order for this magnificent energy to rise within us, it must be kept alive.

Small fires are easily extinguished by strong winds.

These times of upheaval and unrest are more like hurricanes, tornadoes, and earthquakes than just winds. To birth a new foundation here on earth at this time, we have to keep practicing daily, deeply, and perhaps with more conviction and determination than ever before.

Here and now, we have the real chance to align consciously through physical form and become vessels of transformation and divine light.

The fires of spiritual practice, especially over a lifetime, are potent and real. Intentionality—how strongly we hold onto a particular thought or goal—is measurable on an electromagnetic scale and has proven effects in the universal quantum field. When we cultivate and direct our life force—*prana*—biofield - electro-magnetic energy with our hearts, it gathers spiritual force.

Why This Matters Now

Mother Earth is crying *and dying.* Through forests and along coastlines, across the country and from Four Corners and the Anasazi ruins of Colorado and New Mexico through North and South Dakota, pipelines are blowing out the understory of this planet. Our government and our banks fund it. Ecological and emotional balance on the planet depends on us. The middle of the country, including our sacred ruins and Native burial grounds, is for sale to the Army Corps of Engineers, and that could be forever, dear friends.

Earth's sickness is also our own. Now friends, families, and neighbors have cancer or know someone who does. Most of us feel sick or tired much of the time. The pace and demands of life are wearing us out. We've reached a point where almost nobody can see beyond their medical specialists or tech devices anymore.

What better time than *now* to unify and direct our spiritual force?

Let's turn off the news, put away our devices, and unroll our yoga mats. Let's take a few quiet breaths, hearing the sound of the air come and go and the beat of our own hearts. Let's remember to practice and pray together as well; unified group consciousness is the most influential power we know. Through vibrational resonance with ourselves and each other, we create self-organizing fields that transform the reality of our lives. Imagine our world pulsating with explosive human potential, where thoughts, intentions and beliefs serve the healing and good of all. It all starts with a single breath, an open heart, and glimpsing the body's miraculous ability to heal.

The Gods have been calling us to act. The time is now.

ADDITIONAL RESOURCES
AND INFORMATION

Brain Therapy

Brain-Lymph Therapies

Chikly Health Institute: www.chikly.com

Find a therapist: https://chiklyinstitute.com/find-a-therapist

Dr. Chikly and Alaya Chikly bios: https://chiklyinstitute.com/meet-the
-developers

What Is Brain Therapy?

Ann House's YouTube video:

https://www.youtube.com/watch?v=FZ0q0JWRVn4

https://www.youtube.com/watch?v=UltczDDj5aI

https://www.youtube.com/watch?v=FZ0q0JWRVn4&list=PL7o5WA
5N5yzUpKlMo4GWqSmnSfpx2z01

https://www.youtube.com/watch?v=w5tQmB5Sa30&list=PL7o5W
A5N5yzUpKlMo4GWqSmnSfpx2z01_&index=3

Craniosacral Therapy

Upledger Institute: www.upledger.com

Find a therapist: https://www.iahp.com/pages/search/index.php

Dr. John Upledger bio: https://www.upledger.com/about/john-upledger.php

Dr. Mauro Zappaterra: https://www.youtube.com/watch?v=jplHEHYHpfg

CST history: http://www.whitetigernaturalmedicine.com/craniosacral-therapy/history-craniosacral-therapy

http://iacst.ie/history-craniosacral-therapy

Neuromuscular Therapy

https://nmtcenter.com

Judith Walker Delaney bio: https://nmtcenter.com/bio/

Definitions and Links

Biophoton emission in humans

https://www.ncbi.nlm.nih.gov/pubmed/15947465

http://www.greenmedinfo.com/blog/biophotons-human-body-emits-communicates-and-made-light

https://www.ncbi.nlm.nih.gov/pmc/articles/PMC5433113/

Brain Research by the Dalai Lama

https://www.theatlantic.com/health/archive/2015/07/dalai-lama-neuroscience-compassion/397706/

https://www.scientificamerican.com/article/neuroscientists-dalai-lama-swap-insights-meditation/

https://abcnews.go.com/Health/neuroscientist-richie-davidson-dalai-lama-gave-total-wake/story?id=40859233

Detoxification

Aluminum Detox

https://www.naturalhealth365.com/effective-way-to-detox-aluminum-2910.html

EMFs

Nick Pineault talk, "Cell Phone Radiation and the 5G Rollout": https://www.youtube.com/watch?v=a_sreKWeDLU

Dr. Joel Moscowitz, University of Berkeley: https://www.saferemr.com

https://techpinions.com/verizon-to-launch-5g-next-week/44651

https://www.marinij.com/2018/11/01/marin-supervisors-decide-to-join-legal-challenge-to-5g-rollout/

"Zapped" by Dr. Ann Louise Gittleman: https://www.barnesandnoble.com/w/zapped-ann-louise-gittleman/1103373245

GMOs, WIFI, and Chronic Disease: https://www.naturalhealth365.com/gmo-foods-wifi-2962.html

Heavy/Toxic Metals

https://www.thoughtco.com/definition-of-heavy-metal-605190

https://www.lenntech.com/processes/heavy/heavy-metals/heavy-metals.htm

https://en.wikipedia.org/wiki/Heavy_metals

Heavy Metal Detox

www.wendymyers.com

Wendy Myers/Laura Adler detox talk: https://myersdetox.com/myers-detox-podcast-274-how-environmental-toxins-can-mess-with-your-microbiome-with-lara-adler/?utm_campaign=3-14-19_7am_Thursday%20Newsletter_tier1%20%28NQtUw7%29&utm_medium=email&utm_source=tier1_60-days-engagement&_ke=eyJrbF9lbWFpbCI6ICJvbXRhcmFAcXVpZXRtaW5kLmNvbSIsICJrbF9jb21wYW55X2lkIjogIkx4taGNaOCJ9

Ion cleanse detoxifying foot baths: https://www.amajordifference.com/?utm_source=quietmindhealing

Fascia

https://www.youtube.com/watch?v=_FtSP-tkSug

https://www.youtube.com/watch?v=uzy8-wQzQMY

Glia

https://www.ncbi.nlm.nih.gov/pmc/articles/PMC5303749/

https://www.ncbi.nlm.nih.gov/books/NBK10921/

https://www.barnesandnoble.com/s/The+Other+Brain%3A+Douglas+Fields?_requestid=9204743

Head Injuries

http://www.columbianeurology.org/neurology/staywell/document.php?id=33918

(Pay special attention: Symptoms are not always evident immediately; they may manifest progressively over time. Medicine then labels it *brain damage*. Use osteopathic adjustments and craniosacral and brain-lymph therapies to lower inflammation and enable brain flow.)

Heart-Brain Coherence

https://www.heartmath.org/articles-of-the-heart/the-math-of-heart
math/coherence/

https://www.greggbraden.com/blog/meditation-inner-peace
-and-calm/

Nerve Function

Minerals like calcium, sodium, potassium, and chloride change the ionic charge of nerve cells to create the "action potential" that fires the nerve (basic science behind both metabolism and body-as-light).

https://www.verywellmind.com/what-is-an-action-potential-2794811

Nervous System

Autonomic Nervous System (ANS)

Sympathetic vs Parasympathetic: https://www.sciencedaily.com/
terms/sympathetic_nervous_system.htm

Central Nervous System (CNS)

https://www.medicalnewstoday.com/articles/307076.php

Neuroplasticity: https://www.medicinenet.com/script/main/art.
asp?articlekey=40362

Neurogenesis: https://qbi.uq.edu.au/brain-basics/brain-physiology/
what-neurogenesis

Piezoelectric: https://en.wikipedia.org/wiki/Piezoelectricity

PTSD: https://www.mayoclinic.org/diseases-conditions/post-traumatic
-stress-disorder/symptoms-causes/syc-20355967

Quantum Evolution

Throughout history, when threatened with extinction entire species would mutate in a single generation to survive and thrive. With current challenges to global health and peace, many species—ours included—are facing the possibility of extinction now. What if conscious intention can awaken our innate capacity for **quantum evolution** in time?

https://en.wikipedia.org/wiki/Quantum_evolution

Quantum Reality

Quantum reality is beyond the realm of third-dimension time, space, and matter. In this reality, we awaken to infinite options in the quantum field. In quantum reality, anything is possible and everything already exists; we get to decide. This is where yogis, shamans, and mystics engage with life. (My definition.)

Quantum physics researched this: https://www.sciencemag.org/news/2017/10/quantum-experiment-space-confirms-reality-what-you-make-it-0

Here's a YouTube on quantum reality and life: https://www.youtube.com/watch?v=MjGgqcyLpug

Sensitivity Syndromes

HSPs: https://hsperson.com/test/highly-sensitive-test/

Empaths: https://drjudithorloff.com/top-10-traits-of-an-empath/

Hypermobility Disorders/EDS: https://www.amjmed.com/article/S0002-9343(17)30220-6/pdf

https://www.ehlers-danlos.org/what-is-eds/information-on-eds/hypermobile-eds-and-hypermobility-spectrum-disorders/

EDS: https://www.ncbi.nlm.nih.gov/pubmed/18324963

https://www.ncbi.nlm.nih.gov/m/pubmed/25821089/?i=5andfrom=/23407074/related

https://www.ncbi.nlm.nih.gov/m/pubmed/25821094/?i=2andfrom=/25821089/related

https://www.scientificamerican.com/article/people-who-are-double-jointed-are-more-likely-to-be-anxious/

People of Influence and Their Work

Dr. F. Batmanghelidi: https://www.amazon.com/Your-Bodys-Many-Cries-Water/dp/0970245882

https://www.publishersweekly.com/978-0-446-69074-4

Martha Beck: www.marthabeck.com

Gregg Braden: https://www.greggbraden.com/about-gregg-braden/

Dr. Joe Dispenza: https://drjoedispenza.com/pages/about

My favorite three-minute clip by Dr. D: https://www.dropbox.com/s/yp557yxv2x333nh/Dr%20Joe%20Dispenza%203%3A49.MOV?dl=0

Dr. Ann Louise Gittleman: https://annlouise.com/about/

Larry Heisler (advanced bodywork & massage training): www.newjerseymassage.com

Prabhu Nam Kaur Khalsa: https://www.sikhnet.com/gurbani/artist/prabhu-nam-kaur-khalsa

Sat Santokh Singh Khalsa: http://www.satsantokh.com

https://www.3ho.org/community/your-stories/being-person-consciousness

Snatam Kaur: www.snatamkaur.com/ttc-press-release

Dr. Bruce Lipton: www.brucelipton.com

https://www.brucelipton.com/books/biology-of-belief

with Sadvi Saraswati: https://www.youtube.com/watch?v=aQQ3ahXMyvc

Lynne McTaggart: https://lynnemctaggart.com/about/

on group consciousness and human potential: https://www.youtube.com/watch?v=6FYGRztyR24

Rupert Sheldrake: https://www.sheldrake.org

https://www.youtube.com/watch?v=4BYR32N04sE

Andrew Taylor Still: https://shsmo.org/historicmissourians/name/s/still/

Bessel Vanderkolk: https://www.youtube.com/watchv=GWEjnGsLN-0

Global Consciousness Project: http://noosphere.princeton.edu/home_bottom3.html

Heartmath Institute: https://www.heartmath.org

The Institute of Noetic Science: https://en.wikipedia.org/wiki/Institute_of_Noetic_Sciences

Science and Non Duality: http://www.scienceandnonduality.com

ABOUT THE AUTHOR

Yolanda Pritam Hari has studied pain, body structure, and human potential for forty years. Known as "the body whisperer" who seems to magically erase pain, she is Board Certified in bodywork and massage, an experienced yoga therapist, a certified herbalist, and a wellness coach. Yolanda opened Quiet Mind Healing in 1988, with offices now in Lafayette and Albany, CA.

www.quietmind.com

(L) with Rev Joan Steadman, Head Minister at Agape East Bay in Oakland, CA, where I am in ministry practitioner training.

(R) with Rev TJ Woodward, founder of Agape East Bay Spiritual Center in Oakland, the first satellite of Agape International in L.A., CA

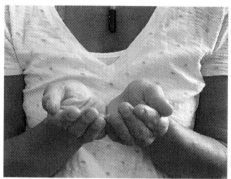

"Thank you for reminding us of the world of blessings and possibilities. May all you do, sing, teach, and create come back to you as God's true divine love and light!

-"Hari Arti" Jana Lynn, The Meditation & Massage Cottage, Lafayette, CA